Brian Lockwood

☞ **W9-AVJ-302**

Learn how to turn data into decisions.

From startups to the Fortune 500, smart companies are betting on data-driven insight, seizing the opportunities that are emerging from the convergence of four powerful trends:

- New methods of collecting, managing, and analyzing data

- Cloud computing that offers inexpensive storage and flexible, on-demand computing power for massive data sets

- Visualization techniques that turn complex data into images that tell a compelling story

- Tools that make the power of data available to anyone

Get control over big data and turn it into insight with O'Reilly's Strata offerings. Find the inspiration and information to create new products or revive existing ones, understand customer behavior, and get the data edge.

O'REILLY®

Visit oreilly.com/data to learn more.

21 Recipes for Mining Twitter

21 Recipes for Mining Twitter

Matthew A. Russell

O'REILLY®

Beijing · Cambridge · Farnham · Köln · Sebastopol · Tokyo

21 Recipes for Mining Twitter
by Matthew A. Russell

Published by O'Reilly Media, Inc., 1005 Gravenstein Highway North, Sebastopol, CA 95472.

O'Reilly books may be purchased for educational, business, or sales promotional use. Online editions are also available for most titles (*http://my.safaribooksonline.com*). For more information, contact our corporate/institutional sales department: (800) 998-9938 or *corporate@oreilly.com*.

Editor:	Mike Loukides	**Cover Designer:**	Karen Montgomery
Production Editor:	Kristen Borg	**Interior Designer:**	David Futato
Proofreader:	Kristen Borg	**Illustrator:**	Robert Romano

Printing History:

February 2011:   First Edition.

ISBN: 978-1-449-30316-7

[LSI]

1296743683

Table of Contents

Preface

Introduction

This intentionally terse recipe collection provides you with 21 easily adaptable Twitter mining recipes and is a spin-off of Mining the Social Web (O'Reilly), a more comprehensive work that covers a much larger cross-section of the social web and related analysis. Think of this ebook as the jetpack that you can strap onto that great Twitter mining idea you've been noodling on—whether it's as simple as running some disposible scripts to crunch some numbers, or as extensive as creating a full-blown interactive web application.

All of the recipes in this book are written in Python, and if you are reasonably confident with any other programming language, you'll be able to quickly get up to speed and become productive with virtually no trouble at all. Beyond the Python language itself, you'll also want to be familiar with `easy_install` (*http://pypi.python.org/pypi/setup tools*) so that you can get third-party packages that we'll be using along the way. A great warmup for this ebook is Chapter 1 (Hacking on Twitter Data) from Mining the Social Web. It walks you through tools like `easy_install` and discusses specific environment issues that might be helpful—and the best news is that you can download a full resolution copy, absolutely free!

One other thing you should consider doing up front, if you haven't already, is quickly skimming through the official Twitter API documentation (*http://dev.twitter.com/doc*) and related development documents linked on that page. Twitter has a very easy-to-use API with a lot of degrees of freedom, and `twitter` (*http://github.com/sixohsix/twit ter*), a third-party package we'll use extensively, is a beautiful wrapper around the API. Once you know a little bit about the API, it'll quickly become obvious how to interact with it using `twitter`.

Finally—enjoy! And be sure to follow @SocialWebMining (*http://twitter.com/Social WebMining*) on Twitter or "like" the Mining the Social Web Facebook page (*http://facebook.com/MiningTheSocialWeb*) to stay up to date with the latest updates, news, additional content, and more.

Conventions Used in This Book

The following typographical conventions are used in this book:

Italic
> Indicates new terms, URLs, email addresses, filenames, and file extensions.

`Constant width`
> Used for program listings, as well as within paragraphs to refer to program elements such as variable or function names, databases, data types, environment variables, statements, and keywords.

`Constant width bold`
> Shows commands or other text that should be typed literally by the user.

`Constant width italic`
> Shows text that should be replaced with user-supplied values or by values determined by context.

 This icon signifies a tip, suggestion, or general note.

 This icon indicates a warning or caution.

Using Code Examples

This book is here to help you get your job done. In general, you may use the code in this book in your programs and documentation. You do not need to contact us for permission unless you're reproducing a significant portion of the code. For example, writing a program that uses several chunks of code from this book does not require permission. Selling or distributing a CD-ROM of examples from O'Reilly books does require permission. Answering a question by citing this book and quoting example code does not require permission. Incorporating a significant amount of example code from this book into your product's documentation does require permission.

We appreciate, but do not require, attribution. An attribution usually includes the title, author, publisher, and ISBN. For example: "*21 Recipes for Mining Twitter* by Matthew A. Russell (O'Reilly). Copyright 2011 Matthew A. Russell, 978-1-449-30316-7."

If you feel your use of code examples falls outside fair use or the permission given above, feel free to contact us at *permissions@oreilly.com*.

Safari® Books Online

Safari Books Online is an on-demand digital library that lets you easily search over 7,500 technology and creative reference books and videos to find the answers you need quickly.

With a subscription, you can read any page and watch any video from our library online. Read books on your cell phone and mobile devices. Access new titles before they are available for print, and get exclusive access to manuscripts in development and post feedback for the authors. Copy and paste code samples, organize your favorites, download chapters, bookmark key sections, create notes, print out pages, and benefit from tons of other time-saving features.

O'Reilly Media has uploaded this book to the Safari Books Online service. To have full digital access to this book and others on similar topics from O'Reilly and other publishers, sign up for free at *http://my.safaribooksonline.com*.

How to Contact Us

Please address comments and questions concerning this book to the publisher:

> O'Reilly Media, Inc.
> 1005 Gravenstein Highway North
> Sebastopol, CA 95472
> 800-998-9938 (in the United States or Canada)
> 707-829-0515 (international or local)
> 707-829-0104 (fax)

We have a web page for this book, where we list errata, examples, and any additional information. You can access this page at:

> *http://oreilly.com/catalog/9781449303167*

To comment or ask technical questions about this book, send email to:

> *bookquestions@oreilly.com*

For more information about our books, courses, conferences, and news, see our website at *http://www.oreilly.com*.

Find us on Facebook: *http://facebook.com/oreilly*

Follow us on Twitter: *http://twitter.com/oreillymedia*

Watch us on YouTube: *http://www.youtube.com/oreillymedia*

The Recipes

1.1 Using OAuth to Access Twitter APIs

Problem

You want to access your own data or another user's data for analysis.

Solution

Take advantage of Twitter's OAuth implementation to gain full access to Twitter's entire API.

Discussion

Twitter currently implements OAuth 1.0a (*http://oauth.net/core/1.0a/*), an authorization mechanism expressly designed to allow users to grant third parties access to their data without having to do the unthinkable—doling out their username and password. Various third-party Python packages such as `twitter` (`easy_install twitter`) provide easy-to-use abstractions for performing the "OAuth dance," so that you can easily implement client programs to walk the user through this process. In the case of Twitter, the first step involved is registering your application with Twitter at *http://dev.twitter .com/apps* where Twitter provides you with a *consumer key* and *consumer secret* that uniquely identify your application. You provide these values to Twitter when requesting access to a user's data, and Twitter prompts the user with information about the nature of your request. Assuming the user approves your application, Twitter then provides the user with a PIN code for the user to give back to you. Using your consumer key, consumer secret, and this PIN code, you retrieve back an *access token* and *access token secret* that ultimately are used to get you the authorization required to access the user's data.

Example 1-1 illustrates how to use the consumer key and consumer secret to do the OAuth dance with the `twitter` package and gain access to a user's data. To streamline future authorizations, the access token and access token secret are written to disk for later use.

Example 1-1. Using OAuth to access Twitter APIs (see http://github.com/ptwobrussell/Recipes-for-Mining-Twitter/blob/master/recipe__oauth_login.py)

```python
# -*- coding: utf-8 -*-

import os
import sys
import twitter

from twitter.oauth import write_token_file, read_token_file
from twitter.oauth_dance import oauth_dance

def oauth_login(app_name='',
                consumer_key='',
                consumer_secret='',
                token_file='out/twitter.oauth'):

    try:
        (access_token, access_token_secret) = read_token_file(token_file)
    except IOError, e:
        (access_token, access_token_secret) = oauth_dance(app_name, consumer_key,
                consumer_secret)

        if not os.path.isdir('out'):
            os.mkdir('out')

        write_token_file(token_file, access_token, access_token_secret)

        print >> sys.stderr, "OAuth Success. Token file stored to", token_file

    return twitter.Twitter(domain='api.twitter.com', api_version='1',
                auth=twitter.oauth.OAuth(access_token, access_token_secret,
                consumer_key, consumer_secret))

if __name__ == '__main__':

    # Go to http://twitter.com/apps/new to create an app and get these items.
    # See also http://dev.twitter.com/pages/oauth_single_token

    APP_NAME = ''
    CONSUMER_KEY = ''
    CONSUMER_SECRET = ''

    oauth_login(APP_NAME, CONSUMER_KEY, CONSUMER_SECRET)
```

Although not necessarily the norm, Twitter has conveniently opted to provide you with direct access to your own access token and access token secret, so that you can bypass the OAuth dance for a particular application you've created under your own account. You can find a "My Access Token" link to these values under your application's details. These should be the same values written to the *twitter.oauth* file in Example 1-1, which ultimately enables you to instantiate the `twitter.Twitter` object without all of the hoopla. Note that while convenient for retrieving your own access data from your own account, this shortcut provides no benefit if your goal is to write a client program for accessing someone else's data. Do the full OAuth dance in that case instead.

See Also

OAuth 2.0 spec (*http://oauth.net/2/*), Authenticating Requests with OAuth (*http://dev .twitter.com/auth*), OAuth FAQ (*http://dev.twitter.com/pages/oauth_faq*)

1.2 Looking Up the Trending Topics

Problem

You want to keep track of the trending topics on Twitter over a period of time.

Solution

Use the /trends resource (*http://dev.twitter.com/doc/get/trends*) to retrieve the list of trending topics along with Python's built-in sleep function, in order to periodically retrieve updates from the /trends resource.

Discussion

The /trends resource returns a simple JSON object that provides a list of the currently trending topics. Examples 1-2 and 1-3 illustrate the approach and sample results.

Example 1-2. Discovering the trending topics (see http://github.com/ptwobrussell/Recipes-for-Mining -Twitter/blob/master/recipe__get_trending_topics.py)

```
# -*- coding: utf-8 -*-

import json
import twitter

t = twitter.Twitter(domain='api.twitter.com', api_version='1')

print json.dumps(t.trends(), indent=1)
```

Example 1-3. Sample results for a trending topics query

```
{
 "trends": [
  {
   "url": "http://search.twitter.com/search?q=Ben+Roethlisberger",
   "name": "Ben Roethlisberger"
  },

  ... output truncated ...

 ],
 "as_of": "Sun, 09 Jan 2011 23:20:30 +0000"
}
```

You can easily extract the names of the trending topics from this data structure with the list comprehension shown in Example 1-4.

Example 1-4. Using a list comprehension to extract trend names from a trending topics query

```
trends = [
            trend['name']
                for trend in t.trends()['trends']
          ]
```

From here, it's a simple matter to archive them to disk as JSON, as shown in Example 1-5.

Example 1-5. Collecting time-series data for trending topics (see http://github.com/ptwobrussell/ Recipes-for-Mining-Twitter/blob/master/recipe__trending_topics_time_series.py)

```
# -*- coding: utf-8 -*-

import os
import sys
import datetime
import time
import json
import twitter

t = twitter.Twitter(domain='api.twitter.com', api_version='1')

if not os.path.isdir('out/trends_data'):
        os.makedirs('out/trends_data')

while True:

    now = str(datetime.datetime.now())

    trends = json.dumps(t.trends(), indent=1)

    f = open(os.path.join(os.getcwd(), 'out', 'trends_data', now), 'w')
    f.write(trends)
    f.close()

    print >> sys.stderr, "Wrote data file", f.name
    print >> sys.stderr, "Zzz..."

    time.sleep(60) # 60 seconds
```

The result of the script is a directory that contains JSON data in files named by time-stamp, and you can read back in the data by opening up a `file` and using the `json.loads` method. Maintaining timestamped archives of tweets for a particular query could work almost identically. Although to keep this example as simple as possible, raw JSON is written to a file, it's not a good practice to build up a directory with many thousands of files in it. Just about any type of key-value store or a simple relational schema with only a single table containing a "key" and "value" column would work just fine. SQLite (*http://www.sqlite.org/*) or CouchDB (*http://couchdb.apache.org/*) are good places to start looking.

See Also

http://docs.python.org/library/sqlite3.html

1.3 Extracting Tweet Entities

Problem

You want to extract tweet entities such as @mentions, #hashtags, and short URLs from search results or other batches of tweets that don't have entities extracted.

Solution

Use the `twitter_text` (*http://github.com/dryan/twitter-text-py*) package's `Extractor` class to extract the tweet entities.

Discussion

As of January 2011, the `/search` resource does not provide any opt-in parameters for the automatic extraction of tweet entities as is the case with other APIs such as the various `/statuses` resources, but you can use `twitter_text` (`easy_install twitter-text-py`) to extract entities in the very same way that Twitter extracts them in production. The `twitter_text` package is implemented to the same specification as the `twitter-text-rb` Ruby gem (*https://github.com/mzsanford/twitter-text-rb*) that Twitter uses on its internal platform. Example 1-6 illustrates a typical usage of `twitter_text`.

Example 1-6. Extracting Tweet entities (see http://github.com/ptwobrussell/Recipes-for-Mining -Twitter/blob/master/recipe__extract_tweet_entities.py)

```
# -*- coding: utf-8 -*-

import json
import twitter_text

def get_entities(tweet):

    extractor = twitter_text.Extractor(tweet['text'])

    # Note: the production Twitter API contains a few additional fields in
    # the entities hash that would require additional API calls to resolve.
    # See API resources that offer the include_entities parameter for details.

    entities = {}
    entities['user_mentions'] = []
    for um in extractor.extract_mentioned_screen_names_with_indices():
        entities['user_mentions'].append(um)
```

```python
    entities['hashtags'] = []
    for ht in extractor.extract_hashtags_with_indices():

        # Massage field name to match production twitter api

        ht['text'] = ht['hashtag']
        del ht['hashtag']
        entities['hashtags'].append(ht)

    entities['urls'] = []
    for url in extractor.extract_urls_with_indices():
        entities['urls'].append(url)

    return entities

if __name__ == '__main__':

    # A mocked up array of tweets for purposes of illustration.
    # Assume tweets have been fetched from the /search resource or elsewhere.

    tweets = \
        [
            {
             'text' : 'Get @SocialWebMining example code at http://bit.ly/biais2 #wOOt'

             # ... more tweet fields ...

            },

            # ... more tweets ...

        ]

    for tweet in tweets:
        tweet['entities'] = get_entities(tweet)

    print json.dumps(tweets, indent=1)
```

Sample results follow in Example 1-7.

Example 1-7. Sample extracted Tweet entities

```
[
 {
  "text": "Get @SocialWebMining example code at http://bit.ly/biais2 #wOOt",
  "entities": {
  "user_mentions": [
   {
    "indices": [
     4,
     20
    ],
    "screen_name": "SocialWebMining"
   }
```

```
    ],
    "hashtags": [
      {
        "indices": [
          58,
          63
        ],
        "text": "w00t"
      }
    ],
    "urls": [
      {
        "url": "http://bit.ly/biais2",
        "indices": [
          37,
          57
        ]
      }
    ]
  }
 }
}
]
```

Whenever possible, use the `include_entities` parameter in requests to have Twitter automatically extract tweet entities for you. But in circumstances where the API resources currently require you to do the heavy lifting, you now know how to easily extract the tweet entities for rapid analysis.

See Also

http://dev.twitter.com/pages/tweet_entities

1.4 Searching for Tweets

Problem

You want to collect a sample of tweets from the public timeline for a custom query.

Solution

Use the `/search` resource to perform a custom query.

Discussion

Example 1-8 illustrates how to use the `/search` resource to perform a custom query against Twitter's public timeline. Similar to the way that search engines work, Twitter's `/search` resource returns results on a per page basis, and you can configure the number of results per page using the `page` and `rpp` (results per page) keyword parameters. As of January 2011, the maximum number of search results that you can retrieve per query is 1,500.

Example 1-8. Searching for tweets by query term (see http://github.com/ptwobrussell/Recipes-for
-Mining-Twitter/blob/master/recipe__search.py)

```
# -*- coding: utf-8 -*-

import sys
import json
import twitter

Q = ' '.join(sys.argv[1])

MAX_PAGES = 15
RESULTS_PER_PAGE = 100

twitter_search = twitter.Twitter(domain="search.twitter.com")

search_results = []
for page in range(1,MAX_PAGES+1):
    search_results += \
        twitter_search.search(q=Q, rpp=RESULTS_PER_PAGE, page=page)['results']

print json.dumps(search_results, indent=1)
```

Example 1-9 displays truncated results for a **StrataConf** query.

Example 1-9. Sample search results for StrataConf

```
[
 {
  "next_page": "?page=2&max_id=24284287591256064&rpp=100&q=StrataConf",
  "completed_in": 0.187719,
  "max_id_str": "24284287591256064",
  "since_id_str": "0",
  "refresh_url": "?since_id=24284287591256064&q=StrataConf",
  "results": [
   {
    "iso_language_code": "en",
    "to_user_id_str": null,
    "text": "RT @ptwobrussell: Generating Dynamic Social Networks...",
    "from_user_id_str": "142175715",
    "profile_image_url": "http://a2.twimg.com/profile_images/1096089942/...",
    "id": 24266314180730880,
    "source": "<a href="http://twitter.com" rel="nofollow">Tweetie for Mac</a>",
    "id_str": "24266314180730880",
    "from_user": "dreasoning",
    "from_user_id": 142175715,
    "to_user_id": null,
    "geo": null,
    "created_at": "Mon, 10 Jan 2011 00:48:34 +0000",
    "metadata": {
    "result_type": "recent"
    }
   },

   ... output truncated ...
```

```
  ],
  "since_id": 0,
  "results_per_page": 100,
  "query": "StrataConf",
  "max_id": 24284287591256064,
  "page": 1
 }
]
```

You can distill the 140 character text field from each tweet in search_results using a list comprehension, as shown in Example 1-10:

Example 1-10. Using a list comprehension to extract tweet text from search results

```
print [ result['text']
        for result in search_results ]
```

Writing out search_results (or just about anything else) to a file as raw JSON with Python's built-in file object is easily accomplished—Example 1-5 includes an overview of how to use file and json.dumps to achieve that end.

It might be the case that you'd like to display some results from a /trends query, and prompt the user for a selection that you feed into the /search resource as a targeted query. Python's built-in raw_input function can be used precisely for this purpose—Example 1-11 shows you how to make it all happen by using raw_input to glue together Example 1-2 and Example 1-8, and then performing a little post-processing with Example 1-6.

Example 1-11. Searching for trending topics (see http://github.com/ptwobrussell/Recipes-for-Mining -Twitter/blob/master/recipe__get_search_results_for_trending_topic.py)

```
# -*- coding: utf-8 -*-

import os
import sys
import json
import twitter
from recipe__extract_tweet_entities import get_entities

MAX_PAGES = 15
RESULTS_PER_PAGE = 100

# Get the trending topics

t = twitter.Twitter(domain='api.twitter.com', api_version='1')

trends = [
            trend['name']
                for trend in t.trends()['trends']
         ]
```

```
idx = 0
for trend in trends:
    print '[%i] %s' % (idx, trend,)
    idx += 1

# Prompt the user

trend_idx = int(raw_input('\nPick a trend: '))

q = trends[trend_idx]

# Search

print >> sys.stderr, 'Fetching tweets for %s...' % (q, )

twitter_search = twitter.Twitter(domain="search.twitter.com")

search_results = []
for page in range(1,MAX_PAGES+1):
    search_results += \
        twitter_search.search(q=q, rpp=RESULTS_PER_PAGE, page=page)['results']

# Extract tweet entities and embed them into search results

for result in search_results:
        result['entities'] = get_entities(result)

if not os.path.isdir('out'):
        os.mkdir('out')

f = open(os.path.join(os.getcwd(), 'out', 'search_results.json'), 'w')
f.write(json.dumps(search_results, indent=1))
f.close()

print >> sys.stderr, "Entities for tweets about trend '%s' saved to %s" % (q, f.name,)
```

See Also

http://dev.twitter.com/doc/get/search, *http://dev.twitter.com/doc/get/trends*

1.5 Extracting a Retweet's Origins

Problem

You want to extract the originating source from a retweet.

Solution

If the tweet's retweet_count field is greater than 0, extract name out of the tweet's user field; also parse the text of the tweet with a regular expression.

Discussion

Although the retweet concept was a grassroots phenomenon that evolved with Twitter's users, the platform has since evolved to natively incorporate retweeting. As a case in point, /status resources in the Twitter platform are now capable of handling a retweet action such that it's no longer necessary to explicitly express the origin of the tweet with conventions such as "RT @user" or "(via @user)" in the 140 character limit. Instead, the tweet itself contains a retweet_count field that expresses the number of times the tweet has been retweeted. If the retweet_count field is greater than 0, it means that the tweet has been retweeted and you should inspect name from the user field encoded into the tweet.

However, keep in mind that even though Twitter's platform now accommodates retweeting at the API level, not all popular Twitter clients have adapted to take advantage of this feature, and there's a lot of archived Twitter data floating around that doesn't contain these fields. Another possibility is that even though someone's Twitter client uses the retweet API, they might also manually annotate the tweet with additional "RT" or "via" criteria of interest. Finally, to throw one more wrench in the gears, note that tweets returned by the /search resource do not contain the retweet_count as of January 2011. Thus, any way you cut it, inspecting the text of the tweet is still a necessity.

Fortunately, a relatively simple regular expression can handle these issues fairly easily. Example 1-12 illustrates a generalized approach that should work well in many circumstances.

Example 1-12. Extracting retweet origins (see http://github.com/ptwobrussell/Recipes-for-Mining -Twitter/blob/master/recipe__get_rt_origins.py)

```
# -*- coding: utf-8 -*-

import re

def get_rt_origins(tweet):

    # Regex adapted from
    # http://stackoverflow.com/questions/655903/python-regular-expression-for-retweets

    rt_patterns = re.compile(r"(RT|via)((?:\b\W*@\w+)+)", re.IGNORECASE)
    rt_origins = []

    # Inspect the tweet to see if it was produced with /statuses/retweet/:id
    # See http://dev.twitter.com/doc/post/statuses/retweet/:id

    if tweet.has_key('retweet_count'):
        if tweet['retweet_count'] > 0:
            rt_origins += [ tweet['user']['name'].lower() ]

    # Also, inspect the tweet for the presence of "legacy" retweet
    # patterns such as "RT" and "via".
```

```python
    try:
        rt_origins += [
                        mention.strip()
                        for mention in rt_patterns.findall(tweet['text'])[0][1].split()
                      ]
    except IndexError, e:
        pass

    # Filter out any duplicates

    return list(set([rto.strip("@").lower() for rto in rt_origins]))

if __name__ == '__main__':

    # A mocked up array of tweets for purposes of illustration.
    # Assume tweets have been fetched from the /search resource or elsewhere.

    tweets = \
    [
        {
        'text' : 'RT @ptowbrussell Get @SocialWebMining at http://bit.ly/biais2 #w00t'

        # ... more tweet fields ...

        },

        {
        'text' : 'Get @SocialWebMining example code at http://bit.ly/biais2 #w00t',
        'retweet_count' : 1,
        'user' : {
         'name' : 'ptwobrussell'

            # ... more user fields ...
        }

        # ... more tweet fields ...

        },

        # ... more tweets ...

    ]

    for tweet in tweets:
        print get_rt_origins(tweet)
```

Although this task is a little bit more complex than it would be in an ideal Twitterverse, the good news is that you're now equipped with a readily reusable routine to take care of the mundane labor, so that you can focus on more interesting analysis and visualization.

See Also

http://blog.programmableweb.com/2010/08/30/twitter-api-adds-retweet-count-and -more/, *http://dev.twitter.com/doc/get/search*, *http://groups.google.com/group/twitter-de velopment-talk/browse_thread/thread/4b08544f2c02d68f*

1.6 Creating a Graph of Retweet Relationships

Problem

You want to construct and analyze a graph data structure of retweet relationships for a set of query results.

Solution

Query for the topic, extract the retweet origins, and then use the NetworkX package to construct a graph to analyze.

Discussion

Recipe 1.4 can be used to assemble a collection of related tweets, and Recipe 1.5 can be used to extract the originating authors, if any, from those tweets. Given these retweet relationships, all that's left is to use the `networkx` (*http://networkx.lanl.gov/*) package (`easy_install networkx`) to construct a directed graph that represents these relation-ships. At the most basic level, nodes on the graph represent the originating authors and retweet authors, while edges convey the `id` of the tweet expressing the relationship. NetworkX contains a slew of useful functions for analyzing graphs that you construct, and Example 1-13 is just about the absolute minimum working example that you'd need to get the gist of how things work.

Example 1-13. Creating a graph using NetworkX

```
# -*- coding: utf-8 -*-

import networkx as nx

g = nx.Graph()

g.add_edge("@user1", "@user2")
g.add_edge("@user1", "@user3")
g.add_edge("@user2", "@user3")
```

Complete details on the *many* virtues of NetworkX can be found in its online docu-mentation, and this simple example is intended only to demonstrate how easy it really is to construct the actual graph once you have the underlying data that you need to represent the nodes in the graph.

Once you have the essential machinery for processing the tweets in place, the key is to loop over the tweets and repeatedly call add_edge on an instance of networkx.Digraph. Example 1-14 illustrates and displays some of the most rudimentary characteristics of the graph.

Example 1-14. Creating a graph of retweet relationships (see http://github.com/ptwobrussell/Recipes-for-Mining-Twitter/blob/master/recipe__create_rt_graph.py)

```python
# -*- coding: utf-8 -*-

import sys
import json
import twitter
import networkx as nx
from recipe__get_rt_origins import get_rt_origins

def create_rt_graph(tweets):

    g = nx.DiGraph()

    for tweet in tweets:

        rt_origins = get_rt_origins(tweet)

        if not rt_origins:
            continue

        for rt_origin in rt_origins:
            g.add_edge(rt_origin.encode('ascii', 'ignore'),
                    tweet['from_user'].encode('ascii', 'ignore'),
                    {'tweet_id': tweet['id']}
            )

    return g

if __name__ == '__main__':

    # Your query

    Q = ' '.join(sys.argv[1])

    # How many pages of data to grab for the search results.

    MAX_PAGES = 15

    # How many search results per page

    RESULTS_PER_PAGE = 100

    # Get some search results for a query.

    twitter_search = twitter.Twitter(domain='search.twitter.com')
    search_results = []
    for page in range(1,MAX_PAGES+1):
```

```
        search_results.append(
            twitter_search.search(q=Q, rpp=RESULTS_PER_PAGE, page=page)
        )

    all_tweets = [tweet for page in search_results for tweet in page['results']]

    # Build up a graph data structure.

    g = create_rt_graph(all_tweets)

    # Print out some stats.

    print >> sys.stderr, "Number nodes:", g.number_of_nodes()
    print >> sys.stderr, "Num edges:", g.number_of_edges()
    print >> sys.stderr, "Num connected components:",
                        len(nx.connected_components(g.to_undirected()))
    print >> sys.stderr, "Node degrees:", sorted(nx.degree(g))
```

Once you have a graph data structure on hand, it's possible to gain lots of valuable insight without the benefit of visualization tools, because some graphs will be too gnarly to visualize in 2D (or even 3D) space. Some options you can explore are searching for cliques in the graph, exploring subgraphs, transforming the graph by applying custom filters that remove nodes or edges, and so on.

1.7 Visualizing a Graph of Retweet Relationships

Problem

You want to visualize a graph of retweets (or just about anything else) with a staple like Graphviz or a JavaScript toolkit such as Protovis.

Solution

Emit DOT language output and convert the output to a static image with Graphviz, or emit JSON output that's consumable by Protovis or your JavaScript toolkit of choice.

Discussion

Recipe 1.6 provides a `create_rt_graph` function that creates a `networkx.DiGraph` instance that can be used as the basis of a DOT language transform or a custom JSON data structure that powers a JavaScript visualization. Let's consider each of these options in turn.

Linux and Unix users could simply emit DOT language output by using `networkx.drawing.write_dot` and then transform the DOT language output into a static image with the `dot` or `circo` utilities on the command line. For example, `circo -Tpng -Otwitter_retweet_graph twitter_retweet_graph.dot` would transform a sample DOT file to a PNG image with the same name.

For Windows users, however, there is some good news and some bad news. The bad news is that networkx.drawing.write_dot raises an ImportError because of underlying C code dependencies, a long-unresolved issue (*https://networkx.lanl.gov/trac/ticket/ 117*). The good news is that it's easily worked around by catching the ImportError and manually emitting the DOT language. With DOT output emitted, standard Graphviz tools can be used normally. Example 1-15 illustrates this.

Example 1-15. Visualizing a graph of retweet relationships with Graphviz (see http://github.com/ ptwobrussell/Recipes-for-Mining-Twitter/blob/master/recipe__visualize_rt_graph_graphviz.py)

```python
# -*- coding: utf-8 -*-

import os
import sys
import twitter
import networkx as nx
from recipe__create_rt_graph import create_rt_graph

# Writes out a DOT language file that can be converted into an
# image by Graphviz.

def write_dot_output(g, out_file):

    try:
        nx.drawing.write_dot(g, out_file)
        print >> sys.stderr, 'Data file written to', out_file
    except ImportError, e:

        # Help for Windows users:
        # Not a general purpose method, but representative of
        # the same output write_dot would provide for this graph
        # if installed and easy to implement.

        dot = ['"%s" -> "%s" [tweet_id=%s]' % (n1, n2, g[n1][n2]['tweet_id'])
                for (n1, n2) in g.edges()]
        f = open(out_file, 'w')
        f.write('''strict digraph {
%s
}''' % (';\n'.join(dot), ))
        f.close()

        print >> sys.stderr, 'Data file written to: %s' % f.name

if __name__ == '__main__':

    # Your query.

    Q = ' '.join(sys.argv[1])

    # Your output.

    OUT = 'twitter_retweet_graph'
```

```
# How many pages of data to grab for the search results.

MAX_PAGES = 15

# How many search results per page.

RESULTS_PER_PAGE = 100

# Get some search results for a query.

twitter_search = twitter.Twitter(domain='search.twitter.com')

search_results = []
for page in range(1,MAX_PAGES+1):

    search_results.append(
        twitter_search.search(q=Q, rpp=RESULTS_PER_PAGE, page=page)
    )

all_tweets = [tweet for page in search_results for tweet in page['results']]

# Build up a graph data structure.

g = create_rt_graph(all_tweets)

# Write Graphviz output.

if not os.path.isdir('out'):
    os.mkdir('out')

f = os.path.join(os.getcwd(), 'out', OUT)

write_dot_output(g, f)

print >> sys.stderr, \
        'Try this on the DOT output: $ dot -Tpng -O%s %s.dot' % (f, f,)
```

As you might imagine, it's not very difficult to emit other types of output formats such as GraphML or JSON. Recipe 1.6 returns a `networkx.DiGraph` instance that can be inspected and used as the basis of a visualization, and emitting JSON output that's consumable in the toolkit of choice is simpler than you might think. Regardless of the specific target output, it's always a predictable structure that encodes nodes, edges, and information payloads for these nodes and edges, as you know from Example 1-15. In the case of Protovis, the specific details of the output are different, but the concept is the very same. Example 1-16 should look quite similar to Example 1-15, and shows you how to get output for Protovis. The Protovis output is an array of node objects and an array of edge objects (see the visualization in Figure 1-1); the edge objects reference the indexes of the node objects to encode source and target information for each edge.

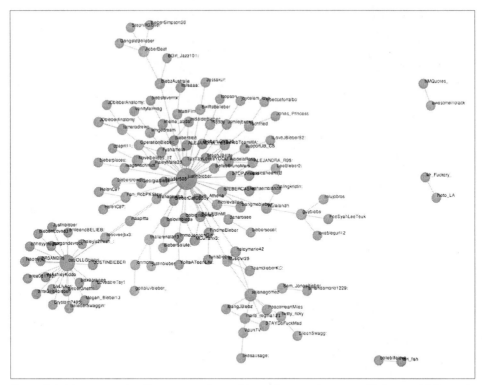

Figure 1-1. It's a snap to visualize retweet relationships and many other types of linkages with Protovis; here, we see the results from a #JustinBieber query

Example 1-16. Visualizing a graph of retweet relationships with Protovis (see http://github.com/ ptwobrussell/Recipes-for-Mining-Twitter/blob/master/recipe__visualize_rt_graph_protovis.py)

```
# -*- coding: utf-8 -*-

import os
import sys
import json
import webbrowser
import twitter
from recipe__create_rt_graph import create_rt_graph

# An HTML page that we'll inject Protovis consumable data into.

HTML_TEMPLATE = 'etc/twitter_retweet_graph.html'
OUT = os.path.basename(HTML_TEMPLATE)

# Writes out an HTML page that can be opened in the browser
# that displays a graph.

def write_protovis_output(g, out_file, html_template):
    nodes = g.nodes()
    indexed_nodes = {}
```

```
    idx = 0
    for n in nodes:
        indexed_nodes.update([(n, idx,)])
        idx += 1

    links = []
    for n1, n2 in g.edges():
        links.append({'source' : indexed_nodes[n2],
                      'target' : indexed_nodes[n1]})

    json_data = json.dumps({"nodes" : [{"nodeName" : n} for n in nodes], \
                            "links" : links}, indent=4)

    html = open(html_template).read() % (json_data,)

    if not os.path.isdir('out'):
        os.mkdir('out')

    f = open(out_file, 'w')
    f.write(html)
    f.close()

    print >> sys.stderr, 'Data file written to: %s' % f.name

if __name__ == '__main__':

    # Your query.

    Q = ' '.join(sys.argv[1])

    # How many pages of data to grab for the search results.

    MAX_PAGES = 15

    # How many search results per page.

    RESULTS_PER_PAGE = 100

    # Get some search results for a query.

    twitter_search = twitter.Twitter(domain='search.twitter.com')

    search_results = []
    for page in range(1,MAX_PAGES+1):

        search_results.append(twitter_search.search(q=Q,
                                                     rpp=RESULTS_PER_PAGE,
                                                     page=page))

    all_tweets = [ tweet
                   for page in search_results
                       for tweet in page['results']
                 ]
```

```
# Build up a graph data structure.

g = create_rt_graph(all_tweets)

# Write Protovis output and open in browser.

if not os.path.isdir('out'):
    os.mkdir('out')

f = os.path.join(os.getcwd(), 'out', OUT)

write_protovis_output(g, f, HTML_TEMPLATE)

webbrowser.open('file://' + f)
```

These simple scripts are merely the beginning of what you could build. Some next steps would be to consider the additional information you could encode into the underlying graph data structure that powers the visualization. For example, you might embed information such the tweet **id** into the graph's edges, or embed user profile information into the nodes. In the case of the Protovis visualization, you could then add event handlers that allow you to view and interact with this data.

See Also

Canviz (*http://code.google.com/p/canviz/*), Graphviz (*http://www.graphviz.org/*), Protovis (*http://vis.stanford.edu/protovis/*), Ubigraph (*http://ubietylab.net/ubigraph/*)

1.8 Capturing Tweets in Real-time with the Streaming API

Problem

You want to capture a stream of public tweets in real-time, optionally filtering by select screen names or keywords in the text of the tweet.

Solution

Use Twitter's streaming API.

Discussion

While handy and quite beautiful, the **twitter** package doesn't support streaming API resources at this time. However, **tweepy** (*http://github.com/joshthecoder/tweepy*) is a very nice package that provides simplified access to streaming API resources and can easily be used to interact with the streaming API. The PyPi version of **tweepy** has been noted to be somewhat dated compared to the latest commit to its public GitHub repository, so it is recommended that you install directly from GitHub using a handy build tool called **pip** (*http://pip.openplans.org/*). You can conveniently and predictably install **pip** with **easy_install pip**, and afterward, a **pip** executable should appear in your path.

From there, you can install the latest revision of tweepy with the following command: `pip install git+git://github.com/joshthecoder/tweepy.git`.

With tweepy installed, Example 1-17 shows you how to create a streaming API instance and filter for any public tweets containing keywords of interest. Try TeaParty or JustinBieber if you want some interesting results from two high velocity communities.

Example 1-17. Filtering tweets using the streaming API (see http://github.com/ptwobrussell/Recipes -for-Mining-Twitter/blob/master/recipe__streaming_api.py)

```python
# -*- coding: utf-8 -*-

import sys
import tweepy
import webbrowser

# Query terms

Q = sys.argv[1:]

# Get these values from your application settings.

CONSUMER_KEY = ''
CONSUMER_SECRET = ''

# Get these values from the "My Access Token" link located in the
# margin of your application details, or perform the full OAuth
# dance.

ACCESS_TOKEN = ''
ACCESS_TOKEN_SECRET = ''

auth = tweepy.OAuthHandler(CONSUMER_KEY, CONSUMER_SECRET)
auth.set_access_token(ACCESS_TOKEN, ACCESS_TOKEN_SECRET)

# Note: Had you wanted to perform the full OAuth dance instead of using
# an access key and access secret, you could have uses the following
# four lines of code instead of the previous line that manually set the
# access token via auth.set_access_token(ACCESS_TOKEN, ACCESS_TOKEN_SECRET).
#
# auth_url = auth.get_authorization_url(signin_with_twitter=True)
# webbrowser.open(auth_url)
# verifier = raw_input('PIN: ').strip()
# auth.get_access_token(verifier)

class CustomStreamListener(tweepy.StreamListener):

    def on_status(self, status):

        # We'll simply print some values in a tab-delimited format
        # suitable for capturing to a flat file but you could opt
        # store them elsewhere, retweet select statuses, etc.
```

```
    try:
        print "%s\t%s\t%s\t%s" % (status.text,
                                  status.author.screen_name,
                                  status.created_at,
                                  status.source,)
    except Exception, e:
        print >> sys.stderr, 'Encountered Exception:', e
        pass

def on_error(self, status_code):
    print >> sys.stderr, 'Encountered error with status code:', status_code
    return True # Don't kill the stream

def on_timeout(self):
    print >> sys.stderr, 'Timeout...'
    return True # Don't kill the stream

# Create a streaming API and set a timeout value of 60 seconds.

streaming_api = tweepy.streaming.Stream(auth, CustomStreamListener(), timeout=60)

# Optionally filter the statuses you want to track by providing a list
# of users to "follow".

print >> sys.stderr, 'Filtering the public timeline for "%s"' % (' '.join(sys.argv[1:]),)

streaming_api.filter(follow=None, track=Q)
```

If you really like twitter, there's no reason you couldn't use twitter and tweepy together. For example, suppose you wanted to implement a bot to retweet any tweet by Tim O'Reilly about Open Government or Web 2.0. In this scenario, you might use tweepy to capture a stream of tweets, filtering on @timoreilly and certain keywords or hashtags, but use twitter to retweet or perform other actions.

Finally, although a slightly less elegant option, it is certainly possible to poll one or more of the /users timeline resources for updates of interest instead of using the streaming API. If you choose to take this approach, be sure to take advantage of the since_id keyword parameter to request only tweets that have been updated since you last checked.

See Also

http://code.google.com/p/twitter-repeater/source/browse/repeater.py

1.9 Making Robust Twitter Requests

Problem

You want to write a long-running script that harvests large amounts of data, such as the friend and follower ids for a very popular Twitterer; however, the Twitter API is inherently unreliable and imposes rate limits that require you to always expect the unexpected.

Solution

Write an abstraction for making `twitter` requests that accounts for rate limiting and other types of HTTP errors so that you can focus on the problem at hand and not worry about HTTP errors or rate limits, which are just a very specific kind of HTTP error.

Discussion

If you write a long running script with no more precautions taken than crossing your fingers, you'll be unpleasantly surprised when you return only to discover that your script crashed. Although it's possible to handle the exceptional circumstances in the code that calls your script, it's arguably cleaner and will save you time in the long run to go ahead and write an extensible abstraction to handle the various types of HTTP errors that you'll encounter. The most common HTTP errors include 401 errors (Not Authorized—probably, someone is protecting their tweets), 503 errors (the beloved "fail whale"), and 420 errors (rate limit enforcement.) Example 1-18 illustrates a `make_twitter_request` function that attempts to handle the most common perils you'll face. In the case of a 401, note that there's nothing you can really do; most other types of errors require using a timer to wait for a prescribed period of time before making another request.

Example 1-18. Making robust Twitter requests (see http://github.com/ptwobrussell/Recipes-for -Mining-Twitter/blob/master/recipe__make_twitter_request.py)

```
# -*- coding: utf-8 -*-

import sys
import time
from urllib2 import URLError
import twitter

# See recipe__get_friends_followers.py for an example of how you might use
# make_twitter_request to do something like harvest a bunch of friend ids for a user.

def make_twitter_request(t, twitterFunction, max_errors=3, *args, **kwArgs):

    # A nested function for handling common HTTPErrors. Return an updated value
    # for wait_period if the problem is a 503 error. Block until the rate limit is
    # reset if a rate limiting issue.

    def handle_http_error(e, t, wait_period=2):

        if wait_period > 3600: # Seconds
            print >> sys.stderr, 'Too many retries. Quitting.'
            raise e
```

```
                if e.e.code == 401:
                    print >> sys.stderr, 'Encountered 401 Error (Not Authorized)'
                    return None
                elif e.e.code in (502, 503):
                    print >> sys.stderr, 'Encountered %i Error. Will retry in %i seconds' % \
                            (e.e.code, wait_period)
                    time.sleep(wait_period)
                    wait_period *= 1.5
                    return wait_period
                elif t.account.rate_limit_status()['remaining_hits'] == 0:
                    status = t.account.rate_limit_status()
                    now = time.time()  # UTC
                    when_rate_limit_resets = status['reset_time_in_seconds']  # UTC
                    sleep_time = when_rate_limit_resets - now
                    print >> sys.stderr, 'Rate limit reached: sleeping for %i secs' % \
                            (sleep_time, )
                    time.sleep(sleep_time)
                    return 2
                else:
                    raise e

        wait_period = 2
        error_count = 0
        while True:
            try:
                return twitterFunction(*args, **kwArgs)
            except twitter.api.TwitterHTTPError, e:
                error_count = 0
                wait_period = handle_http_error(e, t, wait_period)
                if wait_period is None:
                    return
            except URLError, e:
                error_count += 1
                print >> sys.stderr, "URLError encountered. Continuing."
                if error_count > max_errors:
                    print >> sys.stderr, "Too many consecutive errors...bailing out."
                    raise
```

In order to invoke make_twitter_request, pass it an instance of your twitter.Twitter
API, a reference to the function you want to invoke that instance, and any other relevant
parameters. For example, assuming t is an instance of twitter.Twitter, you might
invoke make_twitter_request(t, t.followers.ids, screen_name="SocialWebMining",
cursor=-1) to issue a request for @SocialWebMining's follower ids. Note that you can
(and usually should) capture the returned response and follow the cursor in the event
that you have a request that entails multiple iterations to resolve all of the data.

See Also

http://dev.twitter.com/pages/responses_errors

1.10 Harvesting Tweets

Problem

You want to harvest and store tweets from a collection of `id` values, or harvest entire timelines of tweets.

Solution

Use the `/statuses/show` resource to fetch a single tweet by its `id` value; the various `/statuses/*_timeline` methods can be used to fetch timeline data. CouchDB is a great option for persistent storage, and also provides a map/reduce processing paradigm and built-in ways to share your analysis with others.

Discussion

The `/statuses/show` resource provides a mechanism to fetch a single tweet by its `id` value and does not require authentication although it does enforce rate-limiting by taking the IP address of the request into account. One particularly handy circumstance in which you'll need to fetch single tweets is when you want to reconstruct a discussion thread as specified by an `in_reply_to` field that appears in the tweet, hinting that it's a direct reply to another user. Example 1-19 illustrates how to fetch a tweet.

Example 1-19. Fetching tweets one at a time (see http://github.com/ptwobrussell/Recipes-for-Mining -Twitter/blob/master/recipe__get_tweet_by_id.py)

```
# -*- coding: utf-8 -*-

import sys
import json
import twitter

TWEET_ID = sys.argv[1] # Example: 24877908333961216

t = twitter.Twitter(domain='api.twitter.com', api_version='1')

# No authentication required, but rate limiting is enforced

tweet = t.statuses.show(id=TWEET_ID, include_entities=1)

print json.dumps(tweet, indent=1)
```

 The remainder of this recipe will provide a super-quick overview of the steps involved to get something up and running with CouchDB (*http:// couchdb.apache.org/*). If you're not interested in using CouchDB, it should be easy enough to adapt the core ideas that are presented for your own storage medium of choice.

Although there will be plenty of circumstances when you may want to cherrypick particular tweets from a timeline, it'll more often be the case that you need to harvest a batch of tweets. As the need to harvest batches of tweets increases, your need for an elegant storage medium and framework for processing the tweets will increase accordingly. CouchDB is one option that you should consider as part of your search for an ideal database to house your tweets. Its document-oriented nature is designed so that it can natively store JSON data (the response format from Twitter's API) and its built-in map/reduce (*http://en.wikipedia.org/wiki/MapReduce*) functionality provides a great fabric for many types of tweet analysis that you'll encounter. A full introduction to CouchDB is well beyond this book's scope, but assuming you're able to install a local instance of CouchDB, all that's left is to easy_install couchdb, and make sure the code line below is modified under the [query_servers] of your *local.ini* configuration file. (Make sure it points to the actual location of the couchpy script that is installed on *your* system when you easy_install couchdb.) The effect of this change is that you can install additional *query servers* for languages other than JavaScript (which is the default).

```
[query_servers]
python = /Library/Frameworks/Python.framework/Versions/2.6/bin/couchpy
```

With CouchDB installed and running on your local machine, the couchdb package installed, and your configuration updated to use couchpy as a Python query server, you're all set to use the script presented in Example 1-20 to harvest timeline data and persist it in CouchDB. Once you've run the script, you'll want to use CouchDB's built-in administrative interface (Futon, located at *http://localhost:5984/_utils/*), to view the data in your web browser.

Example 1-20. Harvesting tweets via timelines (see http://github.com/ptwobrussell/Recipes-for -Mining-Twitter/blob/master/recipe__harvest_timeline.py)

```python
# -*- coding: utf-8 -*-

import sys
import time
import twitter
import couchdb
from couchdb.design import ViewDefinition
from recipe__oauth_login import oauth_login
from recipe__make_twitter_request import make_twitter_request


def usage():
    print 'Usage: $ %s timeline_name [max_pages] [screen_name]' % (sys.argv[0], )
    print
    print '\ttimeline_name in [public, home, user]'
    print '\t0 < max_pages <= 16 for timeline_name in [home, user]'
    print '\tmax_pages == 1 for timeline_name == public'
```

```python
    print 'Notes:'
    print '\t* ~800 statuses are available from the home timeline.'
    print '\t* ~3200 statuses are available from the user timeline.'
    print '\t* The public timeline updates every 60 secs and returns 20 statuses.'
    print '\t* See the streaming/search API for additional options to harvest tweets.'

    exit()


if len(sys.argv) < 2 or sys.argv[1] not in ('public', 'home', 'user'):
    usage()
if len(sys.argv) > 2 and not sys.argv[2].isdigit():
    usage()
if len(sys.argv) > 3 and sys.argv[1] != 'user':
    usage()

TIMELINE_NAME = sys.argv[1]
MAX_PAGES = int(sys.argv[2])

USER = None

KW = {  # For the Twitter API call
    'count': 200,
    'skip_users': 'true',
    'include_entities': 'true',
    'since_id': 1,
    }

if TIMELINE_NAME == 'user':
    USER = sys.argv[3]
    KW['screen_name'] = USER
if TIMELINE_NAME == 'home' and MAX_PAGES > 4:
    MAX_PAGES = 4
if TIMELINE_NAME == 'user' and MAX_PAGES > 16:
    MAX_PAGES = 16
if TIMELINE_NAME == 'public':
    MAX_PAGES = 1

# Authentication is needed for harvesting home timelines.
# Don't forget to add keyword parameters to the oauth_login call below
# if you don't have a token file on disk.

t = oauth_login()

# Establish a connection to a CouchDB database.

server = couchdb.Server('http://localhost:5984')
DB = 'tweets-%s-timeline' % (TIMELINE_NAME, )

if USER:
    DB = '%s-%s' % (DB, USER)
```

```
try:
    db = server.create(DB)
except couchdb.http.PreconditionFailed, e:

    # Already exists, so append to it, keeping in mind that duplicates could occur.

    db = server[DB]

    # Try to avoid appending duplicate data into the system by only retrieving tweets
    # newer than the ones already in the system. A trivial mapper/reducer combination
    # allows us to pull out the max tweet id which guards against duplicates for the
    # home and user timelines. It has no effect for the public timeline.


    # For each tweet, emit tuples that can be passed into a reducer to find the maximum
    # tweet value.

    def id_mapper(doc):
        yield (None, doc['id'])


    # Find the maximum tweet id.
    def max_finding_reducer(keys, values, rereduce):
        return max(values)


    view = ViewDefinition('index', 'max_tweet_id', id_mapper, max_finding_reducer,
                          language='python')
    view.sync(db)
    try:
        KW['since_id'] = int([_id for _id in db.view('index/max_tweet_id')][0].value)
    except IndexError, e:
        KW['since_id'] = 1

# Harvest tweets for the given timeline.
# For friend and home timelines, the unofficial limitation is about 800 statuses
# although other documentation may state otherwise. The public timeline only returns
# 20 statuses and gets updated every 60 seconds, so consider using the streaming API
# for public statuses. See http://bit.ly/fgJrAx
# Note that the count and since_id params have no effect for the public timeline

page_num = 1
while page_num <= MAX_PAGES:
    KW['page'] = page_num
    api_call = getattr(t.statuses, TIMELINE_NAME + '_timeline')
    tweets = make_twitter_request(t, api_call, **KW)

    # Actually storing tweets in CouchDB is as simple as passing them
    # into a call to db.update.

    db.update(tweets, all_or_nothing=True)
```

```
    print >> sys.stderr, 'Fetched %i tweets' % (len(tweets),)

    page_num += 1

print >> sys.stderr, 'Done fetching tweets'
```

The ability to query the data you have collected in CouchDB is just a simple map/reduce query away, and it just so happens that Recipe 1.11 provides an example to get you on your way.

See Also

http://couchdb.apache.org/, *http://www.couchone.com/*

1.11 Creating a Tag Cloud from Tweet Entities

Problem

You want to analyze the entities from timeline data (or elsewhere) and display them in a tag cloud to quickly get the gist of what someone is talking about.

Solution

Harvest tweets using an approach such as the one described in Example 1-20 (using the `include_entities` parameter in your query to have entities extracted automatically, if it's available for your API resource), and then build a frequency map that tabulates how many times each entity occurs. Feed this frequency information into one of many tagcloud visualizations—such as WP-Cumulus (*http://wordpress.org/extend/plugins/wp-cumulus/*)—to quickly get a nice visualization of what's happening.

Discussion

Example 1-20 introduces an approach for harvesting tweets using CouchDB, and this recipe continues with that assumption to use CouchDB's map/reduce functionality as an example of a query that you could run on tweets you've stored in CouchDB. Example 1-21 presents a somewhat lengthy code listing that you should skim on a first reading; come back to it after you've seen the visualization in action and take a closer look. The gist is that it computes the frequencies for tweet entities and writes this data into a template so that the WP-Cumulus tag cloud can visualize it. A visualization illustrating this is shown in Figure 1-2. The ensuing discussion should clarify the broad strokes of what is involved.

Figure 1-2. WP-Cumulus is an interactive tag cloud that you can use to get an intuitive visual image of what's going on in a batch of tweets; here, we see results from a #JustinBieber query

Example 1-21. Creating a tag cloud from tweet entities (see http://github.com/ptwobrussell/Recipes -for-Mining-Twitter/blob/master/recipe__tweet_entities_tagcloud.py)

```
# -*- coding: utf-8 -*-

import os
import sys
import webbrowser
import json
from cgi import escape
from math import log
import couchdb
from couchdb.design import ViewDefinition

# Use recipe__harvest_timeline.py to load some data before running
# this script. It loads data from CouchDB, not Twitter's API.

DB = sys.argv[1]

HTML_TEMPLATE = 'etc/tagcloud_template.html'
MIN_FREQUENCY = 2
MIN_FONT_SIZE = 3
MAX_FONT_SIZE = 20
```

```
server = couchdb.Server('http://localhost:5984')
db = server[DB]

# Map entities in tweets to the docs that they appear in.

def entity_count_mapper(doc):
    if not doc.get('entities'):
        import twitter_text

        def get_entities(tweet):

            # Now extract various entities from it and build up a familiar structure.

            extractor = twitter_text.Extractor(tweet['text'])

            # Note that the production Twitter API contains a few additional fields in
            # the entities hash that would require additional API calls to resolve.

            entities = {}
            entities['user_mentions'] = []
            for um in extractor.extract_mentioned_screen_names_with_indices():
                entities['user_mentions'].append(um)

            entities['hashtags'] = []
            for ht in extractor.extract_hashtags_with_indices():

                # Massage field name to match production twitter api.

                ht['text'] = ht['hashtag']
                del ht['hashtag']
                entities['hashtags'].append(ht)

            entities['urls'] = []
            for url in extractor.extract_urls_with_indices():
                entities['urls'].append(url)

            return entities

        doc['entities'] = get_entities(doc)

    # A mapper can, and often does, include multiple calls to "yield" which
    # emits a key, value tuple. This tuple can be whatever you'd like. Here,
    # we emit a tweet entity as the key and the tweet id as the value, even
    # though it's really only the key that we're interested in analyzing.

    if doc['entities'].get('user_mentions'):
        for user_mention in doc['entities']['user_mentions']:
            yield ('@' + user_mention['screen_name'].lower(), doc['id'])

    if doc['entities'].get('hashtags'):
        for hashtag in doc['entities']['hashtags']:
            yield ('#' + hashtag['text'], doc['id'])


# Count the frequencies of each entity.
```

```python
def summing_reducer(keys, values, rereduce):
    if rereduce:
        return sum(values)
    else:
        return len(values)


# Creating a "view" in a "design document" is the mechanism that you use
# to set up your map/reduce query.

view = ViewDefinition('index', 'entity_count_by_doc', entity_count_mapper,
                      reduce_fun=summing_reducer, language='python')

view.sync(db)

entities_freqs = [(row.key, row.value) for row in
                  db.view('index/entity_count_by_doc', group=True)]

# Create output for the WP-Cumulus tag cloud and sort terms by freq along the way.

raw_output = sorted([[escape(term), '', freq] for (term, freq) in entities_freqs
                    if freq > MIN_FREQUENCY], key=lambda x: x[2])

# Implementation details for the size of terms in the tag cloud were adapted from
# http://help.com/post/383276-anyone-knows-the-formula-for-font-s

min_freq = raw_output[0][2]
max_freq = raw_output[-1][2]


def weightTermByFreq(f):
    return (f - min_freq) * (MAX_FONT_SIZE - MIN_FONT_SIZE) / (max_freq
            - min_freq) + MIN_FONT_SIZE


weighted_output = [[i[0], i[1], weightTermByFreq(i[2])] for i in raw_output]

# Substitute the JSON data structure into the template.

html_page = open(HTML_TEMPLATE).read() % \
                (json.dumps(weighted_output),)

if not os.path.isdir('out'):
    os.mkdir('out')

f = open(os.path.join(os.getcwd(), 'out', os.path.basename(HTML_TEMPLATE)), 'w')
f.write(html_page)
f.close()

print >> sys.stderr, 'Tagcloud stored in: %s' % f.name

# Open up the web page in your browser.

webbrowser.open("file://" + f.name)
```

The following discussion is somewhat advanced and focuses on trying to explain how the `summing_reducer` function works, depending on whether the value of its `rereduce` parameter is `True` or `False`. Feel free to skip this section if you're not interested in honing in on those details just yet.

In short, a mapper will take a tweet and emit normalized entities such as #hashtags and @mentions, and a reducer will perform aggregate analysis on those values emitted from the mapper by counting them. The output from multiple mappers is then passed into a reducer for the purpose of performing an aggregate operation. The important subtlety with the way that the reducer is invoked is that it is passed keys and values such that each invocation's values parameter guarantees matching keys. This turns out to be a very convenient characteristic, and for the problem of tabulating frequencies, it means that you only need to count the number of values to know the frequency for the key if the `rereduce` parameter is `False`. In other words, if the keys were `['@user', '@user', '@user']`, you'd only need to compute the length of that list to get the frequency of @user for that particular invocation of the reduction function.

The actual number of keys and values that are passed into each invocation of a reduction function is a function of the underlying B-Tree used in CouchDB, and here, the illustration used a tiny size of 3 for simplicity. The subtlety to note is that multiple calls to the reducer could occur with the same keys—which conceptually means that you wouldn't have a final aggregated answer. Instead you'd end up with something like `[("@user", 3), ("@user", 3), "@user", 3), ...]`, which represents an intermediate result. When this happens, it's necessary for the output of these reductions to be *rereduced*, in which case the `rereduce` flag will be set to `True`. The value for the keys is of no consequence, since we are already operating on output that's guaranteed to have been produced from the same keys. In the working example, all that needs to happen is a *sum* of the values, 3 + 3 + 3 +, ... + 3, in order to come to a final aggregate value. A discussion of `rereduce` is inherently a slightly advanced topic, but is fundamental to an understanding of the map/reduce paradigm. It may bend your brain just a little bit, but manually working through some examples is very conducive to getting the hang of it.

Once the frequency maps are computed, the details for visualizing the entities in a tag cloud amount to little more than scaling the size of each entity and writing out the JSON data structure that the WP-Cumulus tag cloud expects. The `HTML_TEMPLATE` in the example contains the necessary `SCRIPT` tag references to pull the JavaScript libraries and other necessary artifacts. Only the data needs to be written to a `%s` placeholder in the template.

See Also

http://labs.mudynamics.com/wp-content/uploads/2009/04/icouch.html, *http://help.com/post/383276-anyone-knows-the-formula-for-font-s*

1.12 Summarizing Link Targets

Problem

You want to summarize the text of a web page that's indicated by a short URL in a tweet.

Solution

Extract the text from the web page, and then use a natural language processing (NLP) toolkit such as the Natural Language Toolkit (NLTK) to help you extract the most important sentences to create a machine-generated abstract.

Discussion

Summarizing web pages is a very powerful capability, and this is especially the case in the context of a tweet where you have a lot of additional metadata (or "reactions") about the page from one or more tweets. Summarizing web pages is a particularly hard and messy problem, but you can bootstrap a reasonable solution with less effort than you might think. The problem is essentially two-fold: extracting the text from the page, and summarizing the text.

The difficulty of extracting the text from a web page can vary wildly depending on the source and layout of the page. A good starting point is to simply use some out-of-the-box functionality and see if it'll work before taking matters into your own hands. One possible approach is to run the text through NLTK (*http://www.nltk.org/*)'s `clean_html` function (`easy_install nltk`) and then use BeautifulSoup (*http://www.crummy.com/software/BeautifulSoup/*) to decode the HTML entities such as &, <, >, etc., into their English equivalents. In a perfect world, all HTML would be authored such that the content and presentation are perfectly divided, but in reality, you'll hardly ever be lucky enough to work within such ideal conditions. Simple heuristics and pattern matching will get you a long way, and the summarization algorithm that we'll use to summarize the content is fortunately very tolerant of noise and artifacts in the page.

Given some text data, one possible approach to summarization is to develop a heuristic that picks out the most important sentences and return those sentences in the same order that they appeared in the document. All the way back in 1958, H.P. Luhn published an algorithm (*http://portal.acm.org/citation.cfm?id=1662360*) for doing just that by using frequency analysis of the words in the document as the fundamental linchpin of the heuristic. Luhn determined that it is often the case that sentences containing frequently appearing terms are the most important sentences, and the more closely together the frequently appearing terms occur, the better.

Example 1-22 illustrates a routine for fetching a web page, extracting its text, and using Luhn's algorithm to summarize the text in the web page. NLTK is used to segment the sentences into text, and the rest of the routine is fairly algorithmic. Luhn's original paper is well worth a read and provides a very easy-to-understand discussion of this approach.

Example 1-22. Summarizing link targets (see http://github.com/ptwobrussell/Recipes-for-Mining-Twitter/blob/master/recipe__summarize_webpage.py)

```
# -*- coding: utf-8 -*-

import sys
import json
import nltk
import numpy
import urllib2
from BeautifulSoup import BeautifulStoneSoup

URL = sys.argv[1]

# Some parameters you can use to tune the core algorithm.

N = 100  # Number of words to consider
CLUSTER_THRESHOLD = 5  # Distance between words to consider
TOP_SENTENCES = 5  # Number of sentences to return for a "top n" summary

# Approach taken from "The Automatic Creation of Literature Abstracts" by H.P. Luhn.

def _score_sentences(sentences, important_words):
    scores = []
    sentence_idx = -1

    for s in [nltk.tokenize.word_tokenize(s) for s in sentences]:

        sentence_idx += 1
        word_idx = []

        # For each word in the word list...
        for w in important_words:
            try:
                # Compute an index for where any important words occur in the sentence.

                word_idx.append(s.index(w))
            except ValueError, e: # w not in this particular sentence
                pass

        word_idx.sort()

        # It is possible that some sentences may not contain any important words at all.
        if len(word_idx)== 0: continue

        # Using the word index, compute clusters by using a max distance threshold
        # for any two consecutive words.

        clusters = []
        cluster = [word_idx[0]]
        i = 1
        while i < len(word_idx):
```

```
                    if word_idx[i] - word_idx[i - 1] < CLUSTER_THRESHOLD:
                        cluster.append(word_idx[i])
                    else:
                        clusters.append(cluster[:])
                        cluster = [word_idx[i]]
                    i += 1
                clusters.append(cluster)

                # Score each cluster. The max score for any given cluster is the score
                # for the sentence.

                max_cluster_score = 0
                for c in clusters:
                    significant_words_in_cluster = len(c)
                    total_words_in_cluster = c[-1] - c[0] + 1
                    score = 1.0 * significant_words_in_cluster \
                        * significant_words_in_cluster / total_words_in_cluster

                    if score > max_cluster_score:
                        max_cluster_score = score

                scores.append((sentence_idx, score))

        return scores

    def summarize(txt):
        sentences = [s for s in nltk.tokenize.sent_tokenize(txt)]
        normalized_sentences = [s.lower() for s in sentences]

        words = [w.lower() for sentence in normalized_sentences for w in
                    nltk.tokenize.word_tokenize(sentence)]

        fdist = nltk.FreqDist(words)

        top_n_words = [w[0] for w in fdist.items()
                        if w[0] not in nltk.corpus.stopwords.words('english')][:N]

        scored_sentences = _score_sentences(normalized_sentences, top_n_words)

        # Summarization Approach 1:
        # Filter out non-significant sentences by using the average score plus a
        # fraction of the std dev as a filter.

        avg = numpy.mean([s[1] for s in scored_sentences])
        std = numpy.std([s[1] for s in scored_sentences])
        mean_scored = [(sent_idx, score) for (sent_idx, score) in scored_sentences
                        if score > avg + 0.5 * std]

        # Summarization Approach 2:
        # Another approach would be to return only the top N ranked sentences.

        top_n_scored = sorted(scored_sentences, key=lambda s: s[1])[-TOP_SENTENCES:]
        top_n_scored = sorted(top_n_scored, key=lambda s: s[0])

        # Decorate the post object with summaries
```

```
    return dict(top_n_summary=[sentences[idx] for (idx, score) in top_n_scored],
                mean_scored_summary=[sentences[idx] for (idx, score) in mean_scored])


# A minimalist approach or scraping the text out of a web page. Lots of time could
# be spent here trying to extract the core content, detecting headers, footers, margins,
# navigation, etc.

def clean_html(html):
    return BeautifulStoneSoup(nltk.clean_html(html),
                              convertEntities=BeautifulStoneSoup.HTML_ENTITIES).contents[0]

if __name__ == '__main__':
    page = urllib2.urlopen(URL).read()

    # It's entirely possible that this "clean page" will be a big mess. YMMV.
    # The good news is that summarize algorithm inherently accounts for handling
    # a lot of this noise.

    clean_page = clean_html(page)

    summary = summarize(clean_page)

    print "-------------------------------------------------"
    print "              'Top N Summary'"
    print "-------------------------------------------------"
    print " ".join(summary['top_n_summary'])
    print
    print
    print "-------------------------------------------------"
    print "             'Mean Scored' Summary"
    print "-------------------------------------------------"
    print " ".join(summary['mean_scored_summary'])
```

NLTK is an incredibly powerful and useful resource, and it's well worth the time and energy to familiarize yourself with what it can do. Likewise, BeautifulSoup is an indispensible package—you'll be glad you don't have to live without it when processing HTML or XML data. Try running this script on a variety of web pages. It should work especially well for lengthier blog entries or news stories.

1.13 Harvesting Friends and Followers

Problem

You want to harvest all of the friends or followers for a particular user.

Solution

Use the robust make_twitter_request function from Recipe 1.9 to collect all of the friend or follower ids via a long-running process.

Discussion

Twitter provides the /friends/ids and /followers/ids resources that you can use to get up to 5,000 friend or follower ids at a time; a cursor is returned that you can use to iteratively access additional batches of ids until you have them all. It's not terribly uncommon for you to want to fetch all of the friends or followers for a group of users, and for the more popular Twitterers, it'll take more than your 350 requests per-hour rate limit will afford you. For example, 350 requests per hour at 5,000 ids per request works out to be 1.75 million ids per hour. However, some of the most interesting Twitterers have many more than 1.75 million followers. Lady Gaga is one of the most (if not the most) popular, with around 8 million followers. Fetching all of those ids would take about 4.5 hours, which is a bit of a wait, but it's still pretty amazing that you could harvest that much data in less than a business day.

While the make_twitter_request function is certainly a handy abstraction, the use of functools.partial (*http://docs.python.org/library/functools.html*) can be used to layer on some additional sugar to illustrate how you could ultimately create the get_friends_ids and get_followers_ids functions that you've *really* always wanted. Example 1-23 illustrates how to use make_twitter_request in the manner described to fetch some friends and followers ids.

Example 1-23. Harvesting friends and followers (see http://github.com/ptwobrussell/Recipes-for -Mining-Twitter/blob/master/recipe__get_friends_followers.py)

```
# -*- coding: utf-8 -*-

import sys
import twitter
from recipe__make_twitter_request import make_twitter_request
import functools

SCREEN_NAME = sys.argv[1]
MAX_IDS = int(sys.argv[2])

if __name__ == '__main__':

    # Not authenticating lowers your rate limit to 150 requests per hr.
    # Authenticate to get 350 requests per hour.

    t = twitter.Twitter(domain='api.twitter.com', api_version='1')

    # You could call make_twitter_request(t, t.friends.ids, *args, **kw) or
    # use functools to "partially bind" a new callable with these parameters

    get_friends_ids = functools.partial(make_twitter_request, t, t.friends.ids)

    # Ditto if you want to do the same thing to get followers...

    # getFollowerIds = functools.partial(make_twitter_request, t, t.followers.ids)
```

```
cursor = -1
ids = []
while cursor != 0:

    # Use make_twitter_request via the partially bound callable...

    response = get_friends_ids(screen_name=SCREEN_NAME, cursor=cursor)
    ids += response['ids']
    cursor = response['next_cursor']

    print >> sys.stderr, 'Fetched %i total ids for %s' % (len(ids), SCREEN_NAME)

    # Consider storing the ids to disk during each iteration to provide an
    # an additional layer of protection from exceptional circumstances.

    if len(ids) >= MAX_IDS:
        break

# Do something useful with the ids like store them to disk...

print ids
```

Note that once you have all of the `ids` in hand, an additional set of operations is required to resolve the screen names and other basic profile information for these users; see Recipe 1.15 for details. If you don't need all of it for batch analysis, you might consider lazy loading it versus harvesting it all up front.

See Also

http://dev.twitter.com/doc/get/friends/ids, *http://dev.twitter.com/doc/get/followers/ids*

1.14 Performing Setwise Operations on Friendship Data

Problem

You want to operate on collections of friends and followers to answer questions such as "Who isn't following me back?", "Who are my mutual friends?", and "What friends/followers do certain users have in common?".

Solution

Use setwise operations such as the `difference` and `intersection` operations to answer these questions.

Discussion

A set is an unordered collection of items, and basic setwise operations such as `difference` and `intersection` can answer many interesting questions you might have. For example, given the follower `ids` for various users, you could find the followers in common for all of those users by computing the intersection of all of the sets of follower `ids`. Likewise, the intersection of a particular user's friend `ids` and follower `ids` could be interpreted as the user's "mutual friends"—the friends that are following back. Computing who isn't following you back is also just a setwise operation away. Logically, subtracting out any follower `id` that doesn't exist in your friend `ids` (the people you are following) would be the people who aren't following you back. In set operations, this would be called taking the *difference* of your followers from your friends, or mathematically: *Friends - Followers*. Unlike the intersection operator, the difference operator isn't symmetric. In other words the result of *Followers - Friends* does not yield the same result as *Friends - Followers*.

Python 2.6+ directly exposes the built-in set type that you can use to learn more about sets, as shown in Example 1-24.

Example 1-24. Using sets in Python

```
>>> s1 = set([1,2,3])
>>> s2 = set([2,4,5])
>>>  s1.intersection(s2)
set([2])
>>> s1.difference(s2)
set([1, 3])
```

Given that you'll more than likely get to the point of analyzing fairly large amounts of friends and followers with setwise operations, you might find yourself pulling data from a database such as SQLite, performing a set operation in memory with Python, and then storing the result back to your database. While there's nothing necessarily wrong with this approach, you should at least be aware of Redis (*http://redis.io/*), a project that makes this type of computation much more efficient. You might think of Redis as a "data structures server"—it's a key-value store, but the values for each key can be typed. Hashes, lists, sets, and ordered sets are just a few of the possibilities. Redis is trivial to get up and running, written in extremely lean C code, and can perform operations in memory and store the result as another key-value pair. In the case of sets, that means that you can perform intersections and differences directly in Redis and fetch the result in a manner that is dramatically more efficient than fetching data, performing the computation in your own application logic, and then sending data back to whatever you retrieved it for storage.

Full instructions for installing Redis can be found at *http://redis.io/download*, and for Unix users, amounts to little more than a `make` command followed by invoking the `redis-server` binary. Windows users should consult *https://github.com/mythz/Service Stack.Redis*. With a Redis server up and running, it's quite easy to adapt scripts such as Example 1-23 to store friend and follower `ids` for a user in Redis so that Redis can perform the `set` operations. Example 1-25 is an adaptation of Example 1-23 that illustrates one possible approach. Note that you'll also need to `easy_install redis` to get the `redis` package so that you can easily access it from Python.

Example 1-25. Performing setwise operations in Python (see http://github.com/ptwobrussell/Recipes -for-Mining-Twitter/blob/master/recipe__setwise_operations.py)

```
# -*- coding: utf-8 -*-

import sys
import functools
import twitter
import locale
import redis
from recipe__make_twitter_request import make_twitter_request

# A convenience function for consistently creating keys for a
# screen name, user id, or anything else you'd like.

def get_redis_id(key_name, screen_name=None, user_id=None):

    if screen_name is not None:
        return 'screen_name$' + screen_name + '$' + key_name
    elif user_id is not None:
        return 'user_id$' + user_id + '$' + key_name
    else:
        raise Exception("No screen_name or user_id provided to get_redis_id")

if __name__ == '__main__':

    SCREEN_NAME = sys.argv[1]
    MAX_IDS = int(sys.argv[2])

    # Create a client to connect to a running redis-server with default
    # connection settings. It is recommended that you run Redis in
    # "append only mode" -- Search for "appendonly yes" in redis.conf for details.

    r = redis.Redis()

    # Not authenticating lowers your rate limit to 150 requests per hr.
    # Authenticate to get 350 requests per hour.

    t = twitter.Twitter(domain='api.twitter.com', api_version='1')

    # Harvest some friend ids.

    get_friends_ids = functools.partial(make_twitter_request, t, t.friends.ids)

    cursor = -1
    ids = []
    while cursor != 0:

        # Use make_twitter_request via the partially bound callable...

        response = get_friends_ids(screen_name=SCREEN_NAME, cursor=cursor)

        # Add the ids to the set in redis with the sadd (set add) operator.

        rid = get_redis_id('friend_ids', screen_name=SCREEN_NAME)
```

```python
    [ r.sadd(rid, _id) for _id in response['ids'] ]

    cursor = response['next_cursor']

    print >> sys.stderr, \
        'Fetched %i total friend ids for %s' % (r.scard(rid), SCREEN_NAME)

    if r.scard(rid) >= MAX_IDS:
        break

# Harvest some follower ids.

get_followers_ids = functools.partial(make_twitter_request, t, t.followers.ids)

cursor = -1
ids = []
while cursor != 0:

    # Use make_twitter_request via the partially bound callable...

    response = get_followers_ids(screen_name=SCREEN_NAME, cursor=cursor)

    # Add the ids to the set in redis with the sadd (set add) operator.

    rid = get_redis_id('follower_ids', screen_name=SCREEN_NAME)

    [ r.sadd(rid, _id) for _id in response['ids'] ]

    cursor = response['next_cursor']

    print >> sys.stderr, \
        'Fetched %i total follower ids for %s' % (r.scard(rid), SCREEN_NAME)

    if r.scard(rid) >= MAX_IDS:
        break

# Compute setwise operations the data in Redis.

n_friends = r.scard(get_redis_id('friend_ids', screen_name=SCREEN_NAME))

n_followers = r.scard(get_redis_id('follower_ids', screen_name=SCREEN_NAME))

n_friends_diff_followers = r.sdiffstore('temp',
                                    [get_redis_id('friend_ids',
                                    screen_name=SCREEN_NAME),
                                    get_redis_id('follower_ids',
                                    screen_name=SCREEN_NAME)])
r.delete('temp')

n_followers_diff_friends = r.sdiffstore('temp',
                                    [get_redis_id('follower_ids',
                                    screen_name=SCREEN_NAME),
                                    get_redis_id('friend_ids',
                                    screen_name=SCREEN_NAME)])
```

```
    r.delete('temp')

    n_friends_inter_followers = r.sinterstore('temp',
            [get_redis_id('follower_ids', screen_name=SCREEN_NAME),
             get_redis_id('friend_ids', screen_name=SCREEN_NAME)])
    r.delete('temp')

    print '%s is following %s' % (SCREEN_NAME, locale.format('%d', n_friends, True))

    print '%s is being followed by %s' % (SCREEN_NAME, locale.format('%d',
                                          n_followers, True))

    print '%s of %s are not following %s back' % (locale.format('%d',
             n_friends_diff_followers, True), locale.format('%d', n_friends, True),
             SCREEN_NAME)

    print '%s of %s are not being followed back by %s' % (locale.format('%d',
             n_followers_diff_friends, True), locale.format('%d', n_followers, True),
             SCREEN_NAME)

    print '%s has %s mutual friends' \
        % (SCREEN_NAME, locale.format('%d', n_friends_inter_followers, True))
```

Because the people who aren't following someone back often says a lot about the person, the next step in certain analyses is to resolve those ids to screen names for further analysis. Example 1-26 shows you how. Another interesting exercise might be to fetch friends and followers for multiple users and devise similarity metrics for these users based upon their friends, followers, profile information, etc. Analyzing users who have been *listed* via the :user/lists API resources might be another interesting approach to consider in computing similarity.

1.15 Resolving User Profile Information

Problem

You have a collection of ids and need to resolve basic profile information (such as screen names) for these users.

Solution

Use the /users/lookup resource to look up profile information for up to 100 users at a time.

Discussion

The /friends/ids and /followers/ids resources return ids that will ultimately need to be resolved, and the /users/lookup resource provides the most efficient way to access this information via Twitter's API. Example 1-26 shows how to use make_twitter_request to resolve a large batch of ids.

Example 1-26. Resolving user profile information (see http://github.com/ptwobrussell/Recipes-for-Mining-Twitter/blob/master/recipe__get_user_info.py)

```python
# -*- coding: utf-8 -*-

from recipe__oauth_login import oauth_login
from recipe__make_twitter_request import make_twitter_request

# Assume ids have been fetched from a scenario such as the
# one presented in recipe__get_friends_followers.py and that
# t is an authenticated instance of twitter.Twitter

def get_info_by_id(t, ids):

    id_to_info = {}

    while len(ids) > 0:

        # Process 100 ids at a time...

        ids_str = ','.join([str(_id) for _id in ids[:100]])
        ids = ids[100:]

        response = make_twitter_request(t,
                              getattr(getattr(t, "users"), "lookup"),
                              user_id=ids_str)

        if response is None:
            break

        if type(response) is dict:  # Handle Twitter API quirk
            response = [response]

        for user_info in response:
            id_to_info[user_info['id']] = user_info

        return id_to_info

# Similarly, you could resolve the same information by screen name
# using code that's virtually identical. These two functions
# could easily be combined.

def get_info_by_screen_name(t, screen_names):

    sn_to_info = {}

    while len(screen_names) > 0:

        # Process 100 ids at a time...

        screen_names_str = ','.join([str(sn) for sn in screen_names[:100]])
        screen_names = screen_names[100:]
```

```
            response = make_twitter_request(t,
                                   getattr(getattr(t, "users"), "lookup"),
                                   screen_name=screen_names_str)

        if response is None:
            break

        if type(response) is dict:  # Handle Twitter API quirk
            response = [response]

        for user_info in response:
            sn_to_info[user_info['screen_name']] = user_info

        return sn_to_info

if __name__ == '__main__':

    # Be sure to pass in any necessary keyword parameters
    # if you don't have a token already stored on file.

    t = oauth_login()

    # Basic usage...

    info = {}
    info.update(get_info_by_screen_name(t, ['ptwobrussell', 'socialwebmining']))
    info.update(get_info_by_id(t, ['2384071']))

    # Do something useful with the profile information like store it to disk.

    import json
    print json.dumps(info, indent=1)
```

Note that the /users/show resource may only be suitable in some circumstances; it does not require authentication, but only returns information for only one user per request. Given the rate limits, this is quite wasteful in terms of API resources if you have more than one user id that you need to resolve.

See Also

http://dev.twitter.com/doc/get/users/lookup, http://dev.twitter.com/doc/get/users/show

1.16 Crawling Followers to Approximate Potential Influence

Problem

You want to approximate someone's influence based upon their popularity and the popularity of their followers.

Solution

Use a breadth-first traversal to crawl the followers of the user to a reasonable depth, and then count the number of nodes in the graph.

Discussion

A breadth-first traversal (*http://en.wikipedia.org/wiki/Breadth-first_search*) is a common technique for traversing a graph, the implicit data structure that underlies social networks. Given a queue, Q1, containing one or more seed nodes, a breadth-first search systematically visits all of the adjacent nodes (neighbors) for these nodes and places them in another queue, Q2. When Q1 becomes empty, it means that all of these nodes have been visited, and the process repeats itself for the nodes in Q2, with Q1 now being used to keep track of neighbors. Once a suitable depth has been reached, the traversal terminates. A breadth-first traversal is easy to implement, and the neighbors for each node can be stored on disk and later analyzed as a graph. The two characteristics that govern the space complexity of a breadth-first traversal are the depth of the traversal and the average branching factor of each node in the graph. The number of followers for Twitter users varies wildly; all it takes to dramatically effect the average branching factor is a very popular follower, so it would be wise to set an upper threshold.

Example 1-27 illustrates an approach for crawling a user's followers. It recycles logic from Recipe 1.9 to constitute a `get_all_followers_ids` function that takes into account exceptional circumstances, and uses this function in `crawl_followers`—a typical implementation of breadth-first search.

Example 1-27. Crawling a friendship graph (see http://github.com/ptwobrussell/Recipes-for-Mining -Twitter/blob/master/recipe__crawl.py)

```
# -*- coding: utf-8 -*-

import sys
import redis
from recipe__make_twitter_request import make_twitter_request
from recipe__setwise_operations import get_redis_id
from recipe__oauth_login import oauth_login


def crawl_followers(t, r, follower_ids, limit=1000000, depth=2):

    # Helper function

    def get_all_followers_ids(user_id, limit):

        cursor = -1
        ids = []
        while cursor != 0:

            response = make_twitter_request(t, t.followers.ids,
                                    user_id=user_id, cursor=cursor)
```

```
            if response is not None:
                ids += response['ids']
                cursor = response['next_cursor']

            print >> sys.stderr, 'Fetched %i total ids for %s' % (len(ids), user_id)

            # Consider storing the ids to disk during each iteration to provide an
            # an additional layer of protection from exceptional circumstances.

            if len(ids) >= limit or response is None:
                break

        return ids

    for fid in follower_ids:

        next_queue = get_all_followers_ids(fid, limit)

        # Store a fid => next_queue mapping in Redis or other database of choice
        # In Redis, it might look something like this:

        rid = get_redis_id('follower_ids', user_id=fid)
        [ r.sadd(rid, _id) for _id in next_queue ]

        d = 1
        while d < depth:
            d += 1
            (queue, next_queue) = (next_queue, [])
            for _fid in queue:
                _follower_ids = get_all_followers_ids(user_id=_fid, limit=limit)

                # Store a fid => _follower_ids mapping in Redis or other
                # database of choice. In Redis, it might look something like this:

                rid = get_redis_id('follower_ids', user_id=fid)
                [ r.sadd(rid, _id) for _id in _follower_ids ]

                next_queue += _follower_ids

if __name__ == '__main__':

    SCREEN_NAME = sys.argv[1]

    # Remember to pass in keyword parameters if you don't have a
    # token file stored on disk already

    t = oauth_login()

    # Resolve the id for SCREEN_NAME

    _id = str(t.users.show(screen_name=SCREEN_NAME)['id'])

    crawl_followers(t, redis.Redis(), [_id])
```

```
# The total number of nodes visited represents one measure of potential influence.
# You can also use the user => follower ids information to create a
# graph for analysis.
```

The code builds upon the foundation established in Recipe 1.13 and Recipe 1.14, and illustrates how you could use Redis to store the follower ids for users encountered during the breadth-first traversal. However, you could just as easily use any other storage medium. Once your traversal has completed, the total number of nodes in the graph is one indicator of the user's potential influence. For example, if you were given a user id and traversed its follower graph to a depth of 1, you'd have a hub and spoke graph that represents the seed node and its adjacent neighbors. A depth of 2 would represent the user, the user's followers, and the user's followers' followers. Obviously, the higher the depth, the higher the number of nodes in the graph and the higher the potential influence. However, it might be the case that the further out you traverse the graph, the more diverse the users become and the less likely it is that a retweet would occur. It would be interesting to hold a rigorous experiment to investigate this hypothesis.

1.17 Analyzing Friendship Relationships such as Friends of Friends

Problem

You want to create a graph that facilitates the analysis of interesting relationships amongst users, such as friends of friends.

Solution

Systematically harvest all of the friendships for users of interest, and load the data into a graph toolkit like NetworkX that offers native graph operations.

Discussion

Recipe 1.13 demonstrated how to fetch all of the friends or followers for a user of interest, and Recipe 1.16 is a logical extension that you can easily adapt to harvest friends or followers using a breadth-first search. Assuming that you've harvested and stored all of the friendships for a collection of users using one of these options, the core operation that you need in order to create a graph is the add_edge operation that connects two nodes at a time. Optionally, directionality for the edge and additional metadata about the nodes or edges may also be embedded.

Example 1-28 illustrates one possible approach to creating a graph of common friendships amongst a group of users and assumes you might have stored the friendship data in Redis. The end goal of this example is to create a hub and spoke graph of a user and all of this user's friends along with any additional friendships that existing amongst this user's friends. See Recipe 1.6 for an another useful example of using NetworkX to construct a graph of retweet relationships.

Example 1-28. Creating friendship graphs (see http://github.com/ptwobrussell/Recipes-for-Mining -Twitter/blob/master/recipe__create_friendship_graph.py)

```python
# -*- coding: utf-8 -*-

import os
import sys
import networkx as nx
import redis
import twitter

from recipe__setwise_operations import get_redis_id

SCREEN_NAME = sys.argv[1]

t = twitter.Twitter(api_version='1', domain='api.twitter.com')

_id = str(t.users.show(screen_name=SCREEN_NAME)['id'])

g = nx.Graph()       # An undirected graph
r = redis.Redis()

# Compute all ids for nodes appearing in the graph. Let's assume you've
# adapted recipe__crawl to harvest all of the friends and friends' friends
# for a user so that you can build a graph to inspect how these
# friendships relate to one another.

# Create a collection of ids for a person and all of this person's friends.

ids = [_id] + list(r.smembers(get_redis_id('friend_ids', user_id=_id)))

# Process each id in the collection such that edges are added to the graph
# for each of current_id's friends if those friends are also
# friends of SCREEN_NAME. In the end, you get a hub and spoke graph of
# SCREEN_NAME and SCREEN_NAME's friends, but you also see connections that
# existing amongst SCREEN_NAME's friends as well.

for current_id in ids:

    print >> sys.stderr, 'Processing user with id', current_id

    try:
        friend_ids = list(r.smembers(get_redis_id('friend_ids', user_id=current_id)))
        friend_ids = [fid for fid in friend_ids if fid in ids]
    except Exception, e:
        print >> sys.stderr, 'Encountered exception. Skipping', current_id

    for friend_id in friend_ids:
        print >> sys.stderr, 'Adding edge %s => %s' % (current_id, friend_id,)
        g.add_edge(current_id, friend_id)

# Optionally, pickle the graph to disk...
```

```
if not os.path.isdir('out'):
    os.mkdir('out')

f = os.path.join('out', SCREEN_NAME + '-friendships.gpickle')
nx.write_gpickle(g, f)

print >> sys.stderr, 'Pickle file stored in', f
```

To further explain how this example works, let's assume that you have a particular user that you're very interested in: @user. Assuming you've harvested all of @user's friendships and all of the friendships for these friendships (friends of friends), you can create a graph of the common friendships that exist for this entire network— whether or not @user is one of the nodes in the graph. There are many spins and variations that you could integrate into this example, and more types of analysis than could fill a small book. As you add more nodes to the graph and more heuristics to the graph construction algorithm, it only gets more interesting. It's well worth the effort to explore the out-of-the-box features that NetworkX provides and spend a little time harvesting some friendship data to analyze.

1.18 Analyzing Friendship Cliques

Problem

You want to find the friendship cliques in a graph.

Solution

Construct a graph using NetworkX and use its built-in functionality to find the cliques.

Discussion

A clique is a graph (or subgraph) in which every node is connected to every other node. For example, a triangle is an example of a 3-clique since it contains only three nodes and all nodes are connected. Clique detection is a very interesting and highly applicable problem to analyzing social networking relationships. Triangles, approximate cliques, trusses, and other topologies can also turn out to have useful properties for analysis. Example 1-29 illustrates an approach for taking a NetworkX graph and discovering the cliques in it.

Example 1-29. Analyzing friendship cliques (see http://github.com/ptwobrussell/Recipes-for-Mining -Twitter/blob/master/recipe__clique_analysis.py)

```
# -*- coding: utf-8 -*-

import sys
import json
import networkx as nx
```

```
G = sys.argv[1]

g = nx.read_gpickle(G)

# Finding cliques is a hard problem, so this could
# take a while for large graphs.
# See http://en.wikipedia.org/wiki/NP-complete and
# http://en.wikipedia.org/wiki/Clique_problem

cliques = [c for c in nx.find_cliques(g)]

num_cliques = len(cliques)

clique_sizes = [len(c) for c in cliques]
max_clique_size = max(clique_sizes)
avg_clique_size = sum(clique_sizes) / num_cliques

max_cliques = [c for c in cliques if len(c) == max_clique_size]

num_max_cliques = len(max_cliques)

max_clique_sets = [set(c) for c in max_cliques]
people_in_every_max_clique = list(reduce(lambda x, y: x.intersection(y),
                                  max_clique_sets))

print 'Num cliques:', num_cliques
print 'Avg clique size:', avg_clique_size
print 'Max clique size:', max_clique_size
print 'Num max cliques:', num_max_cliques
print
print 'People in all max cliques:'
print json.dumps(people_in_every_max_clique, indent=4)
print
print 'Max cliques:'
print json.dumps(max_cliques, indent=4)
```

For purposes of illustration, Mining the Social Web (*http://oreilly.com/catalog/ 0636920010203/*) (O'Reilly) included an analysis conducted in mid-2010 that determined the following statistics for Tim O'Reilly's ~700 friendships:

```
Num cliques:                    762573
Avg clique size:                    14
Max clique size:                    26
Num max cliques:                     6
Num people in every max clique:     20
```

Some of the more interesting insight from the analysis was that there are six different cliques of size 26 in Tim O'Reilly's friendships, which means that those six variations of 26 people all "know" one another to the point that they were at least interested in receiving each other's status updates in their tweet stream. Perhaps even more interesting is that there are 20 people who appeared in all 6 of those maximum cliques. As an example of practical application, if you wanted to get Tim's attention at a conference or Maker event, but can't seem to track him down, you might start looking for one of these other people since there's more than a reasonable likelihood that they're closely connected with him.

As a more technical aside, be advised that finding cliques is a *hard* problem in both a figurative sense, but also in the computational sense that it's a problem that belongs to a class of problems that are known as NP-Complete (*http://en.wikipedia.org/wiki/NP-complete*). In layman's terms, being NP-Complete means that the combinatorics of the problem, whether it be finding cliques or otherwise, grow explosively as the size of the input for the problem grows. Practically speaking, this means that for a very large graph, you either need to wait a *very* long time to get an exact answer to the problem of finding cliques, or you need to be willing to settle for an approximate solution. The implementation that NetworkX offers should work fine on commodity hardware for graphs containing high-hundreds to low-thousands of nodes (possibly even higher) before the time required to compute cliques becomes unbearable.

See Also

http://networkx.lanl.gov/reference/generated/networkx.algorithms.clique.find_cliques.html, *http://en.wikipedia.org/wiki/Clique_problem*

1.19 Analyzing the Authors of Tweets that Appear in Search Results

Problem

You want to analyze user profile information as it relates to the authors of tweets that appear in search results.

Solution

Use the /search resource to fetch search results, and then extract the from_user field from each search result object to look up profile information by screen name using either the /users/show or /users/lookup resources.

Discussion

Unfortunately, there's a long-lived bug (*http://code.google.com/p/twitter-api/issues/detail?id=214*) with the Twitter API's /search resource; the basic problem is that the user id values in search results do not correspond to user id values that you can use with other APIs such as the various /user resources. This means that you have to perform many more requests to resolve profile information for users whose tweets appear in your search results than would ideally be the case. One approach you can take to overcoming this problem is to extract the from_user field in each search result object and use the /users/lookup resource to resolve profile information for up to 100 tweet authors with a single request. Given a collection of targeted search results and corresponding profile information for the authors of those tweets, you can easily build up useful indices (such as screen names to tweet ids, or screen names to location information) as it appears in profiles.

Example 1-30 demonstrates some logic that gets you started along this very path: it searches for a topic of interest, fetches the profile information for authors associated with those tweets, and exposes some useful indices such as a "screen name to location" index that could then be geocoded and visualized on a map to determine if there is a correlation between a tweet author's home location and topics which that user discusses.

Example 1-30. Analyzing the authors of tweets that appear in search results (see http://github.com/ptwobrussell/Recipes-for-Mining-Twitter/blob/master/recipe__analyze_users_in_search_results.py)

```python
# -*- coding: utf-8 -*-

import sys
import twitter
from recipe__get_user_info import get_info_by_screen_name
from recipe__oauth_login import oauth_login

def analyze_users_in_search_results(t, q, max_pages=15, results_per_page=100):

    # Search for something

    search_api = twitter.Twitter(domain="search.twitter.com")
    search_results = []
    for page in range(1,max_pages+1):
        search_results += \
            search_api.search(q=q, rpp=results_per_page, page=page)['results']

    # Extract the screen names (the "from_user" field) from the results
    # and optionally map them to a useful field like the tweet id
    # See http://code.google.com/p/twitter-api/issues/detail?id=214 for
    # why you can't use the user id values.

    screen_name_to_tweet_ids = {}
    for result in search_results:

        screen_name = result['from_user']

        if not screen_name_to_tweet_ids.has_key(screen_name):
            screen_name_to_tweet_ids[screen_name] = []

        screen_name_to_tweet_ids[screen_name] += [ result['id'] ]


    # Use the /users/lookup resource to resolve profile information for
    # these screen names.

    screen_name_to_info = get_info_by_screen_name(t, screen_name_to_tweet_ids.keys())

    # Extract the home location for each user. Note that the "location" field can
    # be anything a user has typed in, and may be something like "Everywhere",
```

```
# "United States" or something else that won't geocode to a specific coordinate
# on a map.

screen_name_to_location = dict([(sn, info['location'])
                                for sn, info in screen_name_to_info.items()])

# Use the various screen_name_to{tweet_ids, info, location} maps to determine
# interesting things about the people who appear in the search results.

return screen_name_to_info, screen_name_to_location, screen_name_to_tweet_ids

if __name__ == '__main__':

    Q = ' '.join(sys.argv[1:])

    # Don't forget to pass in keyword parameters if you don't have
    # a token file stored to disk

    t = oauth_login()

    sn2info, sn2location, sn2tweet_ids = analyze_users_in_search_results(t, Q)

    # Go off and do interesting things...
```

1.20 Visualizing Geodata with a Dorling Cartogram

Problem

You want to visualize geolocation information (for example, the location field from user profile information, included in a batch of tweets such as a search query), in order to determine if there is a correlation between location and some other criterion.

Solution

Devise a heuristic to extract the state from the location information in user profiles and visualize it with a Dorling Cartogram.

Discussion

A Dorling Cartogram (*http://vis.stanford.edu/protovis/ex/cartogram.html*) is essentially a bubble chart where each bubble corresponds to a geographic area such as a state, and each bubble is situated as close as possible to its actual location on a map without overlapping with any other bubbles (see Figure 1-3). Since the size and/or color of each bubble can be used to represent meaningful things, a Dorling Cartogram can give you a very intuitive view of data as it relates to geographic boundaries or regions of a larger land mass. The Protovis toolkit comes with some machinery for creating Dorling Cartograms for locations in the United States, and one interesting example of something that you could do builds upon Recipe 1.19, which demonstrated an approach that you could use to analyze the users who authored tweets from a targeted query.

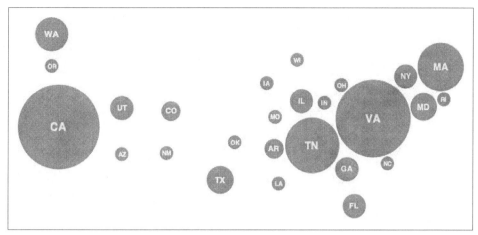

Figure 1-3. A Dorling Cartogram allows you to associate geographic areas with at least two intuitive variables by taking advantage of size and color in the visualization

The thought is that you might attempt to resolve the `location` field in the user profiles for users who have tweets appearing in a focused query, and visualize them on a map in order to determine whether there is any geographic correlation between topics and locations. Of course, it's not quite that simple, since you need to account for the relative population of any given area through some kind of normalization. For example, you might find that a highly populated state like California almost always has the highest number of people talking about any given topic.

Example 1-31 illustrates how to recycle some code from previous recipes and produce a map of state abbreviations and frequency values that correspond to the number of users from a particular state who appear in targeted search results.

Example 1-31. Visualizing geodata with a Dorling Cartogram (see http://github.com/ptwobrussell/ Recipes-for-Mining-Twitter/blob/master/recipe__dorling_cartogram.py)

```
# -*- coding: utf-8 -*-

import os
import sys
import re
import shutil
import json
import webbrowser
import twitter
from recipe__oauth_login import oauth_login
from recipe__analyze_users_in_search_results import analyze_users_in_search_results

# A simple heuristic function that tries to detect the presence of a state
# in a short blurb of text by searching for the full state name and the
# state abbreviation in a suitable context. It returns a map of state
# abbreviations and frequencies. Much more sophisticated alternatives could
# be applied; this is simply a starting point to get you on your way.
```

```python
def get_state_frequencies(locations):

    state_names_to_abbrevs = \
        dict([
            ('ALABAMA', 'AL'),
            ('ALASKA', 'AK'),
            ('ARIZONA', 'AZ'),
            ('ARKANSAS', 'AR'),
            ('CALIFORNIA', 'CA'),
            ('COLORADO', 'CO'),
            ('CONNECTICUT', 'CT'),
            ('DELAWARE', 'DE'),
            ('FLORIDA', 'FL'),
            ('GEORGIA', 'GA'),
            ('HAWAII', 'HI'),
            ('IDAHO', 'ID'),
            ('ILLINOIS', 'IL'),
            ('INDIANA', 'IN'),
            ('IOWA', 'IA'),
            ('KANSAS', 'KS'),
            ('KENTUCKY', 'KY'),
            ('LOUISIANA', 'LA'),
            ('MAINE', 'ME'),
            ('MARYLAND', 'MD'),
            ('MASSACHUSETTS', 'MA'),
            ('MICHIGAN', 'MI'),
            ('MINNESOTA', 'MN'),
            ('MISSISSIPPI', 'MS'),
            ('MISSOURI', 'MO'),
            ('MONTANA', 'MT'),
            ('NEBRASKA', 'NE'),
            ('NEVADA', 'NV'),
            ('NEW HAMPSHIRE', 'NH'),
            ('NEW JERSEY', 'NJ'),
            ('NEW MEXICO', 'NM'),
            ('NEW YORK', 'NY'),
            ('NORTH CAROLINA', 'NC'),
            ('NORTH DAKOTA', 'ND'),
            ('OHIO', 'OH'),
            ('OKLAHOMA', 'OK'),
            ('OREGON', 'OR'),
            ('PENNSYLVANIA', 'PA'),
            ('RHODE ISLAND', 'RI'),
            ('SOUTH CAROLINA', 'SC'),
            ('SOUTH DAKOTA', 'SD'),
            ('TENNESSEE', 'TN'),
            ('TEXAS', 'TX'),
            ('UTAH', 'UT'),
            ('VERMONT', 'VT'),
            ('VIRGINIA', 'VA'),
            ('WASHINGTON', 'WA'),
            ('WEST VIRGINIA', 'WV'),
            ('WISCONSIN', 'WI'),
            ('WYOMING', 'WY')
        ])
```

```python
    state_abbrevs = state_names_to_abbrevs.values()

    states_freqs = dict([(abbrev, 0) for abbrev in state_abbrevs])

    for location in locations:
        if location is None:
            continue

        for name, abbrev in state_names_to_abbrevs.items():
            if location.upper().find(name) > -1:
                states_freqs[abbrev] += 1
                break

            if re.findall(r'\b(' + abbrev + r')\b', location, re.IGNORECASE):
                states_freqs[abbrev] += 1
                break

    return states_freqs

Q = ' '.join(sys.argv[1:])

# Don't forget to pass in keyword parameters if you don't have
# a token file stored to disk.

t = oauth_login()

_, screen_name_to_location, _ = analyze_users_in_search_results(t, Q)
locations = screen_name_to_location.values()

# Resolve state abbreviations to the number of times these states appear.
states_freqs = get_state_frequencies(locations)

# Munge the data to the format expected by Protovis for Dorling Cartogram.

json_data = {}
for state, freq in states_freqs.items():
    json_data[state] = {'value': freq}

# Copy over some scripts for Protovis...
# Our html template references some Protovis scripts, which we can
# simply copy into out/

if not os.path.isdir('out'):
    os.mkdir('out')

shutil.rmtree('out/dorling_cartogram', ignore_errors=True)
shutil.rmtree('out/protovis-3.2', ignore_errors=True)

shutil.copytree('etc/protovis/dorling_cartogram',
                'out/dorling_cartogram')

shutil.copytree('etc/protovis/protovis-3.2',
                'out/protovis-3.2')
```

```
html = open('etc/protovis/dorling_cartogram/dorling_cartogram.html').read() % \
        (json.dumps(json_data),)

f = open(os.path.join(os.getcwd(), 'out', 'dorling_cartogram',
                        'dorling_cartogram.html'), 'w')
f.write(html)
f.close()

print >> sys.stderr, 'Data file written to: %s' % f.name
webbrowser.open('file://' + f.name)
```

1.21 Geocoding Locations from Profiles (or Elsewhere)

Problem

You want to geocode information in tweets for situations beyond what the /geo and /status resources currently support.

Solution

Use the geopy package to perform your own geocoding against your web service of choice, such as Google Maps.

Discussion

You should first consult the capabilities of Twitter's /geo resources and the potential geolocation information that may be embedded into /status resources to make sure that you're aware of the possibilities offered by the Twitter API, but if neither of these options are satisfying enough, then consider taking matters into your own hands with the geopy package (easy_install geopy). Twitter's /geo resources provides several useful capabilities, but (somewhat) surprisingly, nothing that's capable of performing direct geocoding—taking a location such as "Franklin, TN" and resolving it to a co-ordinate. Furthermore, while some users may optionally tweet with geolocation information embedded into their tweets, it's more often the case that users won't enable this option. The current status quo leaves a fairly wide opportunity for geo analysis by way of third-party packages such as geopy.

For example, you might want to search or collect a filtered stream of tweets for a particular topic of interest, and try to determine if there is a correlation between people who are talking about these topics and their location as indicated in their profile information (as demonstrated in Recipe 1.19) with a Dorling Cartogram. While the location field in profile information is a custom text value that could be anything from "Franklin, TN" to "IN UR FRIDGE. EATIN UR FOODZ", be advised that a reasonable number of users do seem to include sensible values that can be geocoded.

Example 1-32. Geocoding locations from profiles (or elsewhere); see http://github.com/ptwobrussell/ Recipes-for-Mining-Twitter/blob/master/recipe__geocode_profile_locations.py

```
# -*- coding: utf-8 -*-

import sys
from urllib2 import HTTPError
import geopy
from recipe__oauth_login import oauth_login
from recipe__analyze_users_in_search_results import analyze_users_in_search_results

def geocode_locations(geocoder, locations):

    # Some basic replacement transforms may be necessary for geocoding services to
    # function properly. You may probably need to add your own as you encounter rough
    # edges in the data or with the geocoding service you settle on. For example, ...

    replacement_transforms = [('San Francisco Bay', 'San Francisco')]

    location_to_coords = {}
    location_to_description = {}

    for location in locations:

        # Avoid unnecessary I/O with a simple cache.

        if location_to_coords.has_key(location):
            continue

        xformed_location = location

        for transform in replacement_transforms:

            xformed_location = xformed_location.replace(*transform)

        while True:

            num_errors = 0

            try:
                # This call returns a generator.

                results = geocoder.geocode(xformed_location, exactly_one=False)
                break
            except HTTPError, e:
                num_errors += 1
                if num_errors >= MAX_HTTP_ERRORS:
                    sys.exit()
                print >> sys.stderr, e.message
                print >> sys.stderr, 'A urllib2 error. Retrying...'
            except UnicodeEncodeError, e:
                print >> sys.stderr, e
                print >> sys.stderr, 'A UnicodeEncodeError...', e.message
                break
```

```
            except geopy.geocoders.google.GQueryError, e:
                print >> sys.stderr, e
                print >> sys.stderr, 'A GQueryError', e.message
                break


        for result in results:

            # Each result is of the form ("Description", (X,Y))
            # Unless you have a some special logic for picking the best of many
            # possible results, choose the first one returned in results and move
            # along.

            location_to_coords[location] = result[1]
            location_to_description[location] = result[0]
            break

    # Use location_to_coords and other information of interest to populate a
    # visualization. Depending on your particular needs, it is highly likely that
    # you'll want to further post process the geocoded locations to filter out
    # location such as "U.S.A." which will plot a placemarker in the geographic
    # center of the United States yet make the visualization look skewed in favor
    # of places like Oklahoma, for example.

    return location_to_coords, location_to_description

if __name__ == '__main__':

    # Use your own API key here if you use a geocoding service
    # such as Google or Yahoo!

    GEOCODING_API_KEY = sys.argv[1]

    Q = ' '.join(sys.argv[2:])

    MAX_HTTP_ERRORS = 100

    g = geopy.geocoders.Google(GEOCODING_API_KEY)

    # Don't forget to pass in keyword parameters if you don't have
    # a token file stored to disk.

    t = oauth_login()

    # This function returns a few useful maps. Let's use the
    # screen_name => location map and geocode the locations.

    _, screen_name_to_location, _ = analyze_users_in_search_results(t, Q, 2)

    locations = screen_name_to_location.values()
    location2coords, location2description = geocode_locations(g, locations)
```

Once you've successfully resolved location descriptions to geocoordinates, you can easily create a KML file and visualize the locations in Google Maps or Google Earth.

The information you need, when and where you need it.

With Safari Books Online, you can:

Access the contents of thousands of technology and business books

- Quickly search over 7000 books and certification guides
- Download whole books or chapters in PDF format, at no extra cost, to print or read on the go
- Copy and paste code
- Save up to 35% on O'Reilly print books
- **New!** Access mobile-friendly books directly from cell phones and mobile devices

Stay up-to-date on emerging topics before the books are published

- Get on-demand access to evolving manuscripts.
- Interact directly with authors of upcoming books

Explore thousands of hours of video on technology and design topics

- Learn from expert video tutorials
- Watch and replay recorded conference sessions

O'REILLY®

Get even more for your money.

Join the O'Reilly Community, and register the O'Reilly books you own. It's free, and you'll get:

- $4.99 ebook upgrade offer
- 40% upgrade offer on O'Reilly print books
- Membership discounts on books and events
- Free lifetime updates to ebooks and videos
- Multiple ebook formats, DRM FREE
- Participation in the O'Reilly community
- Newsletters
- Account management
- 100% Satisfaction Guarantee

Signing up is easy:

1. **Go to: oreilly.com/go/register**
2. **Create an O'Reilly login.**
3. **Provide your address.**
4. **Register your books.**

Note: English-language books only

To order books online:

oreilly.com/store

For questions about products or an order:

orders@oreilly.com

To sign up to get topic-specific email announcements and/or news about upcoming books, conferences, special offers, and new technologies:

elists@oreilly.com

For technical questions about book content:

booktech@oreilly.com

To submit new book proposals to our editors:

proposals@oreilly.com

O'Reilly books are available in multiple DRM-free ebook formats. For more information:

oreilly.com/ebooks

O'REILLY®

Spreading the knowledge of innovators | oreilly.com

CPSIA information can be obtained at www.ICGtesting.com
Printed in the USA
266773BV00003B/6/P